D0579106

This book is a gift from Lancaster Baptist
Church. If you would like to order
additional copies, please visit
strivingtogether.com.

REVIVAL
GOD'S WAY
EMBRACING GOD'S PLAN FOR REVIVAL

John Goetsch

Striving Together Publications
4020 E. Lancaster Blvd.
Lancaster, CA 93535
800.201.7748

Edited by Danielle Mordh
Cover design by Andrew Jones
Layout by Craig Parker

ISBN 978-1-59894-036-7

Printed in the United States of America

Table of Contents

Preface

Growing up on a dairy farm in southern Wisconsin, I was an introvert in every way. With my sister being three years older and my brother nine years younger, I developed my own imaginary world of friends, activities, and dreams. I loved the wide-open spaces the farm afforded, and being alone on a tractor in the middle of a field was like heaven to me. Talking to people scared me, and being in front of people was a disaster, as anyone who witnessed my first piano recital can attest!

School was tolerable because it afforded me the opportunity to play ball. I loved all sports and had some success in football and basketball by the time I reached high school and college. I never went to parties, never dated, had only one or two close friends, and was set to pursue a career in the computer industry. I was more than content to sit in an office somewhere by myself and work with data for the rest of my life.

Through a series of physical setbacks that placed me in the hospital for a three-month period, God began to work in my life. Fearing that He would kill me if I did not surrender, I decided to go to Bible college for a year until I was well enough to transfer somewhere to play football. Had you suggested preaching as a life-calling to me at that time, I would have laughed you out of my presence.

It wasn't that I didn't like preachers or preaching—I did! As a kid, I especially enjoyed the preaching of evangelists. Maybe it was because my dad was saved under an evangelist's ministry in a six-week long revival that made evangelistic services special to our family. We always attended those meetings in our own church as well as some in nearby churches. When I was about ten years old, we attended a John R. Rice revival in the old Turner Hall building in Watertown, Wisconsin. I sat in awe of the large crowd that had gathered, the beautiful singing, and the powerful preaching. I also remember the tears in my dad's eyes as he removed some anti-revival literature from underneath the windshield wiper of our car after the service that night.

There is no doubt in my mind now that God was using those events in my life to prepare me for revival work. Oh, it was a shock when God called me to preach after my second year of Bible college, and time stood still in my heart when He called me to evangelism a year later! In my mind, I did not fit the normal profile of an evangelist. I was awkward with people, afraid to stand before a crowd, and just didn't have the "suave appearance" that I thought all good preachers inherited at birth.

With humanism and modernism creeping into the world and into the church, I knew that there was a need for preaching. I wasn't afraid of hard work and sacrifice, and to me the challenge of seeing another Great Awakening in this world for Christ was energizing. I knew God had called me, and I claimed His promise in 1 Thessalonians 5:24: *"Faithful is he that calleth you, who also will do it."*

In 1978, a mentor of mine, Dr. B. Myron Cedarholm, gave me a book by Dr. John R. Rice entitled *The Evangelist.* My heart burned as I read the following:

> There is a wicked, Christ-denying, unbelieving slander abroad in the land. I hear it everywhere I go. It disgusts me, and I believe it nauseates God. It is the lament of powerless preachers. It is the alibi of dry-eyed Christian workers, without passion, without burden, without tears. It is the prattle of

Bible teachers who never have revivals and who rarely win a soul.

The slander is this: "Well, it is getting harder to win souls all the time." Or stated another way: "We can't have great revivals like Finney and Moody and Torrey and Chapman, and Billy Sunday had."

That is a doctrine of the devil. It minimizes the power of the Gospel. It pictures God as old and weak, unable to cope with the increasing wickedness of the world. It ties the hands of preachers. It makes prayer seem useless. It closes the door of faith. It belittles the love and grace of God. It would make the gates of Hell prevail against churches.

I say again, it is a doctrine of Satan, a lie, an alibi that the enemy of souls puts in the prating mouths of those who do not pay the price to win sinners.

The trouble is not with the harvest but with the reapers. Men are lost but they can be saved. Hearts are hard but they can be broken with the Gospel. Sinners are blinded, sinners are enslaved by Satan, sinners are even dead in trespasses and sins, but Christ has opened blind eyes and released the captives and raised the dead before. Sinners are always lost, always hardened and blinded and enslaved. The basic facts about the Gospel have never changed. Around the world, in all ages and lands, the harvest has been white and the laborers few. The harvest is white today.

In any local situation where the Gospel is continually preached, some people become hardened. But while some individuals become hardened in sin, grow old and die, their places are continually filled by tender-hearted children and young people ready to hear the Gospel. And where one is hardening by hearing the Gospel and rejecting it, another is tendered by the death of loved ones or other merciful dealings of God.

In any particular community there may be times of sowing and then times of reaping, an ebb and flow of opportunity. That has been true in all ages and it is not different today. But around the world it is continually the same: multitudes of people are ripe for the Gospel and could be won by Spirit-filled, impassioned and zealous soul winners. The world is white to the harvest. It always has been and always will be as long as human hearts are what they are and sin is what it is and the Gospel is what it is. THERE IS NO TROUBLE WITH THE HARVEST; THE TROUBLE IS WITH THE REAPERS.

Let's say again that the trouble is not with the harvest. The harvest is white. Souls are lost. Conscience still burns and accuses in the hearts of countless sinners. Millions wonder if they will ever see their loved ones again. The fear of death and Hell and judgment torments many an unconverted sinner, if he hears Spirit-filled Gospel preaching or witnessing. When the Gospel seed is sown, there is some wayside, there is some stony ground, there is some ground covered with thorns and weeds; but there is still much ground where the seed will bring forth fruit, some thirty, some sixty, and some an hundredfold. The trouble is not with the grain; it is with the sower. It is not with the harvest; it is with the reapers. The trouble is not with the sinners; it is with the saints.

In 2 Chronicles 7:14, at the dedication of the Temple of Solomon, the Lord gave a blessed promise of eternal meaning. It is God's way to have a revival, whether among Jews or among Gentiles. The Lord said to Solomon: *"If my people, which are called by my name, shall humble themselves, and pray, and seek my face, and turn from their wicked ways; then will I hear from heaven, and will forgive their sin, and will heal their land."* (*The Evangelist* Dr. John R. Rice, Sword of the Lord Publishing, TN, 1968, pp. 153–155. Murfreesboro, Tennessee.)

Nothing has changed about the Gospel and the harvest since those words were written. Unfortunately, very little has changed among God's people either. Apathy, indifference, worldliness, and anti-evangelism theology have invaded our churches and have left the world lost and in the clutch of Satan's grasp. We need revival! But we need revival *God's way*! It is my prayer that as you read the following pages, God will be able to start that next Great Awakening with you!

CHAPTER ONE

What Makes Us Holy?

All things are lawful unto me, but all things are not expedient: all things are lawful for me, but I will not be brought under the power of any. Meats for the belly, and the belly for meats: but God shall destroy both it and them. Now the body is not for fornication, but for the Lord; and the Lord for the body. And God hath both raised up the Lord, and will also raise up us by his own power. Know ye not that your bodies are the members of Christ? shall I then take the members of Christ, and make them the members of an harlot? God forbid. What? know ye not that he which is joined to an harlot is one body? for two, saith he, shall be one flesh. But he that is joined unto the Lord is one spirit. Flee fornication. Every sin that a man doeth is

*without the body; but he that committeth fornication
sinneth against his own body. What? know ye not
that your body is the temple of the Holy Ghost which
is in you, which ye have of God, and ye are not your
own? For ye are bought with a price: therefore glorify
God in your body, and in your spirit, which are God's.*
—1 CORINTHIANS 6:12–20

Take a moment to look over the cover of your Bible.
As you look, you'll notice written on the front are the
words "Holy Bible." What is it that makes your Bible
holy? Why isn't it just called "The Bible"?

The land of Israel is referred to as the "Holy Land."
What sets Israel apart from the lands surrounding it? I
have visited Israel, and there is nothing very unusual
about Israel's terrain. The land is primarily desert,
filled with rocks and lifeless landscapes. I've walked
the streets of several cities in Israel, and I've seen crime
and a land filled with that which is vile and corrupt—a
land of political unrest. What then, makes the little
country of Israel holy?

The city of Jerusalem is often referred to as
the "Holy City." I have also visited Jerusalem. I have
seen the streets of Old Jerusalem and the streets of
New Jerusalem. I've seen the Hebrew University. I've
watched children play, and I've witnessed crime as
Israeli soldiers walked the streets with machine guns
protecting their people. What makes Jerusalem a holy
city?

The country of Israel and the city of Jerusalem are holy because they belong to God. The "Holy Bible" is not man's Book; man did not write it, preserve it, or inspire it. It is God's Book. That is why it is holy. Israel is God's land, given by God to His people. The city of Jerusalem is God's city. It is where He will one day come and rule and reign for one thousand years upon this earth during the Millennium. The Bible, Israel, and Jerusalem are holy because they belong to God.

First Corinthians 6:19–20 reveals something else that belongs to God, "*What? know ye not that your body is the temple of the Holy Ghost which is in you, which ye have of God, and ye are not your own? For ye are bought with a price: therefore glorify God in your body, and in your spirit, which are God's.*" If you are a child of God, if you have been saved from Hell by the blood of Christ, then you are not your own. You belong to God. And, because you belong to God, you are to be holy.

How holy is your life? How holy is your walk? How holy are your words? How holy are your thoughts? First Corinthians 3:16 shows the seriousness of this subject, "*Know ye not that ye are the temple of God, and that the Spirit of God dwelleth in you? If any man defile the temple of God, him shall God destroy; for the temple of God is holy, which temple ye are.*" God wants to live in a clean house, and He wants to use a clean vessel.

Years ago, I was preaching at a revival meeting. Between Sunday school and church, a man, lady, and three boys walked in and sat in the back row. The pastor leaned over and asked, "Did you see that family that just walked in?" I said, "Yes." He said, "His name is Fred and her name is Kathy. He claims to be saved; she makes no claim of salvation. I'm so glad that they're here."

When I began preaching, I realized what the pastor had told me was probably correct. The man had his Bible open, and he listened with interest. The lady, however, never looked up or at the verse of Scripture. Anyone could see the bitterness on her face; she was a sullen character, obviously not wanting to be there.

After the service that morning, the pastor asked, "Brother Goetsch, would you go with me to visit that family? I'm glad they came, but I'm afraid they won't come back unless we encourage them. Would you go with me?"

After agreeing to his request, we got into his car and headed into the country. We began talking for a while, and in the middle of one of our conversations, he pulled into a driveway. I thought, "We missed the house and are just turning around because this certainly couldn't be the place we are visiting!"

When we were about a hundred yards down the driveway, I saw what looked like a haunted house. The house had not been painted in years. The grass was overgrown, and there were junk piles of cars and car parts everywhere. The house looked as if it would collapse at any moment—one slam of the door, and the whole structure seemed like it would crumble. I thought we had made a mistake; we must have gone too far. But the pastor continued driving down the driveway. As we were getting out of the car, I couldn't believe people actually lived in this house.

The pastor knocked on the door, and I took a step back, thinking the house might cave in. Within a couple moments, one of the boys opened the door and said, "Pastor, come in." The pastor walked in, and I was relieved he went first. I basically had to follow his every step. As we headed into the living room, I looked from side to side and realized there was nowhere to walk except a little path that went through the room. There were things stacked up waist-high on both sides—newspapers, junk, toys, and clothing.

We made it into the dining room and Fred, from the kitchen said, "We're back here!" Frankly, that was the only place they could be. The dining room looked the same way with stuff stacked everywhere—old furniture, leftover dirty dishes, and junk thrown on tables and chairs. When we reached the kitchen, Fred said, "Have a seat." He shooed the cat from the chair that I was supposed to sit on. I hesitantly sat down in that kitchen—a place that smelled of animals, remains of animals, spoiled food and trash. I remember sitting in that house thinking, "How can people live here?"

I wonder, as God makes His way through your heart, if He is thinking, "How in the world am I going to live here?" When He walks through the confines of your mind and soul does He wonder how He is going to reside there? Leviticus 10:10 says, "*And that ye may put difference between holy and unholy, and between unclean and clean.*" Jesus said in John 15:19, "*If ye were of the world, the world would love his own: but because ye are not of the world, but I have chosen you out of the world....*" First Peter 2:9 states, "*But ye are a chosen generation, a royal priesthood, an holy nation, a peculiar people....*" Paul reminds us in Ephesians 5:11, "*And have no fellowship with the unfruitful works of darkness....*" Why? Because God says, "*be ye holy; for I am holy.*"

People today say, "I don't like all these rules. I don't like all these standards. I don't like being told what I can and can't do. We just need to ease up a little." Friend, we cannot be too strict or too narrow-minded when Jesus said in Matthew 5:48, "*Be ye therefore perfect, even as your Father which is in heaven is perfect.*" Our Father wants us to mirror His image—to follow in His likeness.

In a world where sin and riotous living are prevalent, God calls us to holiness. If you are a child of God, you belong to Him. You have been bought with a price and have been commanded to glorify God in your life. Throughout Scripture, God's desire for our holiness is clear, and we can see four timeless truths about His call to turn away from unrighteousness and to turn toward holy living.

An Opposite Revealed

In 1 Corinthians 6:9–10, we see opposite lifestyles to the holy living God commands us to live. The Bible states, *"Know ye not that the unrighteous shall not inherit the kingdom of God? Be not deceived: neither fornicators, nor idolaters, nor adulterers, nor effeminate, nor abusers of themselves with mankind, Nor thieves, nor covetous, nor drunkards, nor revilers, nor extortioners, shall inherit the kingdom of God."*

A Sampling of Depravity

God has given us a list or a sample of wickedness, corruption, and evil. By no means is this a complete list of sins, but God has given us a sample of such depravity. These examples show where all of us could end up as a result of our sin nature. It is the opposite of what God desires for every person. The Bible tells us in the beginning of 1 Corinthians 6:9, *"Know ye not that the unrighteous shall not inherit the kingdom of God?"* Anything that is not right is unrighteous. The standard of righteousness is God, not us. The standard is His perfection, His holiness, His purity; it is not society, not our culture, not what the world says, nor what the church member thinks. It is anything that is not right in comparison to God.

First John 5:17 says, *"All unrighteousness is sin...."* Paul said in 1 Corinthians 15:34, *"Awake to righteousness, and sin not...."* Before we start patting ourselves on the back, remember what Proverbs 24:9 says, *"The thought of foolishness is sin...."* Are you battling with thoughts of criticism, jealousy, worry, or bitterness? Are you struggling with any thoughts of pride? Even the thought of foolishness is sin.

A Separation from the Divine

What separates us from the Divine? 1 Corinthians 6:9 says, *"Know ye not that the unrighteous shall not inherit the kingdom of God?"* Our sin divides us from God.

We forget in the twenty-first century culture that God is holy. We easily compare ourselves with the guy next door or the new convert sitting in the pew next to us. We compare ourselves to the rapist, murderer, or thief we read about in the newspaper. When we hear about a depraved soul and think to ourselves, "Hey, I'm doing just fine," we forget that God is holy. The Bible says in Psalm 5:4–6, *"For thou art not a God that hath pleasure in wickedness: neither shall evil dwell with thee. The foolish shall not stand in thy sight: thou hatest all workers of iniquity. Thou shalt destroy them that speak leasing: the LORD will abhor the bloody and deceitful man."*

Isaiah 59:1–2 says, *"Behold, the LORD's hand is not shortened, that it cannot save; neither his ear heavy, that it cannot hear: But your iniquities have separated between you and your God, and your sins have hid his face from you, that he will not hear."* The wages of sin is eternal separation from God in a place called Hell—a lake of fire and brimstone. Sin's price is deathly high, and many are willing to pay for it because they don't understand the consequences, nor do they understand their alternative choice.

An Omnipotent Redemption

The Bible is very clear regarding the bad news of our sin nature, but I'm glad that God, in His Word, is equally plain about the good news of redemption! I like that word *omnipotent*. It is a theological word that simply means "all-powerful." It refers to God—for He is the only omnipotent One. He is the all-powerful One. While sin holds all of us in its powerful grip, our omnipotent God is more powerful than Satan and can break sin's grip—providing the way of salvation.

A Universal Jeopardy

First Corinthians 6:11 describes a universal jeopardy, *"And such were some of you...."* In this passage, Paul is writing to the local church in Corinth. He's writing to New Testament believers, and he's saying, *"such were some of you."* They had been thieves, adulterers, abusers of themselves with mankind, and drunkards;

but now they are in this local New Testament church in Corinth.

The truth is, because we are all sinners, we are all in a universal jeopardy. It doesn't matter what kind of sin has seeped into our lives or what depravity we have slipped into; the Bible says we are all sinners. The psalmist said in Psalm 51:5, *"Behold, I was shapen in iniquity; and in sin did my mother conceive me."* Paul in Ephesians 2:3 said, *"...we all had our conversation in times past in the lusts of our flesh, fulfilling the desires of the flesh and of the mind; and were by nature the children of wrath, even as others."* We all have sinned, and our sin causes us to come short of the glory of God. *"But we are all as an unclean thing, and all our righteousnesses are as filthy rags; and we all do fade as a leaf; and our iniquities, like the wind, have taken us away"* (Isaiah 64:6). You see, we are all in the same boat. In fact, James 2:10 says, *"For whosoever shall keep the whole law, and yet offend in one point, he is guilty of all."*

An Undeniable Justification

Those sinners to whom Paul was speaking in the church of Corinth—those who were previously involved in thievery, adultery, and an effeminate lifestyle—had now been washed, justified, and redeemed by the blood of the Lamb. First Corinthians 6:11 says, *"And such were some of you: but ye are washed, but ye are sanctified, but ye are justified in the name of the Lord Jesus, and by the Spirit of our God.*" This is an undeniable justification!

Years ago, I was preaching in a college town. On Sunday night, several students from the university came to the meeting. At the close of invitation time, a young man named Jim came forward, shook the pastor's hand at the front, and said, "I want to talk to him," as he was pointing to me. The pastor had him sit down on the front row.

At the end of the service, the pastor whispered to me, "That man on the front row wants to talk to you." When the service was dismissed, I went down and sat next to him, introduced myself, and asked how I could help him.

He began to weep. I moved toward him, put my arm around him, and patted him on the shoulder. "Jim, it's all right," I said, "You don't have to worry about your tears. It's okay. Whenever you're ready to talk, I'm here." He tried to speak, but he couldn't. He just kept weeping. I kept patting him on the back, doing my best to console him.

Finally, he began to wipe his tears and said, "I'm a homosexual." I slowly removed my arm from around him and tried to scoot unnoticeably away. He looked at me, and he said, "You hate me, don't you?"

"No, Jim, I don't. God doesn't either. He hates your sin, but He loves you."

"I ought to be stoned. They ought to take me out of here and just kill me. My sin is abominable in the sight of God! They ought to just kill me today!"

Soon I realized that this man was repenting of his sin. He had the right attitude about sin. He saw his sin in the sight of a holy God. What a joy it was to open my Bible to 1 Corinthians 6 and show him that his particular sin was listed. I explained to him how the believers in Corinth had been plagued by the same sin, but they were washed, sanctified, and justified in the name of the Lord Jesus. They were not saved by a church or a religion or some good deed, but by the precious blood of Christ. What a joy it was to see Jim that night get on his knees and trust Christ as his Saviour.

Now, Jim is in Heaven rejoicing with God. Why? He is rejoicing because God's undeniable justification reached out to him too. We read these words in Romans 5:8, *"God commendeth his love toward us, in that, while we were yet sinners, Christ died for us."* Second Corinthians 8:9 says, *"For ye know the grace of our Lord Jesus Christ, that, though he was rich, yet for your sakes he became poor, that ye through his poverty might be rich."* Romans 5:1 says, *"Therefore being justified by faith, we have peace with God through our Lord Jesus Christ."* Galatians 3:13 says, *"Christ hath redeemed us from the curse of the law, being made a curse for us: for it is written, Cursed is every one that hangeth on a tree."* Isaiah 53:5 says, *"But he was wounded for our transgressions, he was bruised for our iniquities: the chastisement of our peace was upon him; and with his stripes we are healed."* First Peter 1:18–19 says, *"Forasmuch as ye know that ye were not redeemed with corruptible things, as silver and gold, from your vain conversation received by tradition from your fathers; but with the precious blood of Christ, as of a lamb without blemish and without spot:"* God's power is revealed in our lives when we are freed from the bondage of sin and we are redeemed through the blood of Jesus Christ.

An Ownership Restored

When you trust Christ as your personal Saviour an ownership is restored. First Corinthians 6:19–2 says, *"What? know ye not that your body is the temple of the Holy Ghost which is in you, which ye have of God, and ye are not your own? For ye are bought with a price: therefore glorify God in your body, and in your spirit, which are God's."*

A Stolen Identity

When God created us, He created us in His image. The Bible says in Genesis 1:26–27, *"And God said, Let us make man in our image, after our likeness…So God created man in his own image, in the image of God created he him; male and female created he them."* When

God created the human race, He created it in His image; that is, God created man perfect.

Genesis 3 records a specific crime—a case of stolen identity. In Genesis 1 and 2, God says He created man in His own image. In Genesis 3:1–7, the Bible says, "*Now the serpent was more subtil than any beast of the field which the LORD God had made. And he said unto the woman, Yea, hath God said, Ye shall not eat of every tree of the garden? And the woman said unto the serpent, We may eat of the fruit of the trees of the garden: But of the fruit of the tree which is in the midst of the garden, God hath said, Ye shall not eat of it, neither shall ye touch it, lest ye die. And the serpent said unto the woman, Ye shall not surely die: For God doth know that in the day ye eat thereof, then your eyes shall be opened, and ye shall be as gods, knowing good and evil. And when the woman saw that the tree was good for food, and that it was pleasant to the eyes, and a tree to be desired to make one wise, she took of the fruit thereof, and did eat, and gave also unto her husband with her; and he did eat. And the eyes of them both were opened, and they knew that they were naked….*"

Adam and Eve had been created in God's image; they were perfect the way God had created them. But now Satan had stolen that identity. You and I were also deceived with sin and robbed of that same identity as we came into this life. Romans 5:12 says, "*Wherefore, as by one man sin entered into the world, and death by sin; and so death passed upon all men, for that all have sinned:*"

And John 1:12 says, *"But as many as received him, to them gave he power to become the sons of God, even to them that believe on his name:"*

Our identity and ownership can once again be restored to Christ. First Corinthians 6:15 says, *"Know ye not that your bodies are the members of Christ…?"* When we receive Christ as our Saviour, our identity is restored with Him. Second Corinthians 5:17 says, *"Therefore, if any man be in Christ, he is a new creature: old things are passed away; behold, all things are become new."* We are members of His body, of His flesh, and of His bones. Romans 7:4 says, *"Wherefore, my brethren, ye also are become dead to the law by the body of Christ; that ye should be married to another, even to him who is raised from the dead, that we should bring forth fruit unto God."*

Today could be your wedding day. You were once created in Christ's image, but the devil stole that identity through sin. Jesus Christ died on the Cross in order to restore your identity with Him. He wants you to come into a relationship with Him. This could be your wedding day with Christ—a day to spiritually identify and to become one with Him.

A Serious Indebtedness

When we choose to identify with Christ, we accept a spiritual identity—the Spirit of God dwells within us.

Our body is the dwelling place, the home of the Spirit of God. John 14:17 says, "*Even the Spirit of truth; whom the world cannot receive, because it seeth him not, neither knoweth him: but ye know him; for he dwelleth with you, and shall be in you.*" We are not in the flesh but in the Spirit. Because we as Christians have a spiritual identity and the Spirit's indwelling, we have a serious indebtedness.

First Corinthians 6:12 says, "*All things are lawful unto me, but all things are not expedient: all things are lawful for me, but I will not be brought under the power of any.*" Why? Because I'm saved! I've been washed; I've been justified; I've been sanctified; and as a result of my spiritual identity, I have a serious indebtedness.

Animals are not naturally clean; they are disgustingly dirty. I was raised on a dairy farm, and my job was to clean up after our animals. From ages five to eighteen, I spent more hours than I could count standing in the gutter of the barn. The gutter was basically the cows' toilet. We didn't have automated barn cleaners (unless they were called children). I remember spending a lot of time in that gutter throwing manure into the manure spreader, cleaning the calf pens, the hog pens, and the chicken coops.

When I came into the house, I was not allowed in unless I removed my shoes first. I would enter through the cellar door, walk down the steps that led into the cellar, take off my shoes and place them on the cellar stairs. Then I would walk up the stairs that led into the kitchen. Because of the dirt and filth on my shoes, I did not belong in the house.

There were many times when I wanted to go into the house with my shoes on. I would get thirsty halfway through the morning, and sometimes I would need a drink to restore my energy. During those "desperate" times of thirst, I would carefully open the cellar door, walk up the stairs from the cellar, and begin to tiptoe toward the kitchen. I would carefully step on each stair leading toward the kitchen—trying not to make a sound. I would open the door just enough to see if my mother was there. If the kitchen looked empty, I'd tiptoe across the floor and get a drink out of the refrigerator or grab a couple of cookies out of the cookie jar.

Was I sneaky? Yes. Did I get caught? Yes. If my mom didn't catch me personally, the kitchen floor always revealed the evidence. My shoes always gave me away by what they left behind on our kitchen floor.

As children of God, we have been purchased with Christ's blood. But are we still entering His presence with manure on our boots? Are we trying to sneak in our worship with God with the stench of the world still upon us? Are we trying to sneak into our prayer closets? Are we trying to sneak in with our Bible reading? Are we trying to sneak through our service for God in areas of teaching and soulwinning with the world still on our boots? May we take our indebtedness seriously, and may we strive to serve God from pure hearts.

An Obedience Required

First Corinthians 6:20 says, "*For ye are bought with a price: therefore glorify God in your body, and in your spirit, which are God's.*" Because we are children of God who have been justified, sanctified, and bought with a price, our obedience is required!

A Growing Walk

First Corinthians 10:31 says, "*Whether therefore ye eat, or drink, or whatsoever ye do, do all to the glory of God.*" A growing walk shows itself outwardly, but our outward walk will never be right until our hearts—our inward lives—are clean before God. When we allow the Holy Spirit to convict and cleanse us from within, some things will be made right on the outside, as well. We will have the desire to please Christ in everything we do and say. We will have a growing walk—outwardly. As we respond properly to the Holy Spirit who indwells us and as we grow on the inside, we will have the desire to glorify God outwardly with our daily lives just as 1 Corinthians 10:31 commands. The contents of our hearts will be displayed outwardly.

The outward expressions of our inward faith should be characterized by constant growth. Second Peter 3:18 says, *"But grow in grace, and in the knowledge of our Lord and Saviour Jesus Christ...."*

A Glowing Worship

We must glorify God in our walk and also in our worship. Colossians 3:22 says, *"...in singleness of heart, fearing God."*

When one of my friends, Dr. Mark Rasmussen, was growing up, his mother oftentimes reminded him of the Rasmussen name. Before they went to church, ate dinner with a pastor's family, or had guests over to their house, Mrs. Rasmussen would get little Mark in front of her and say, "Now, Mark, you are a Rasmussen. Act like a Rasmussen."

Dr. Rasmussen's father was the pastor of a church. He lived his life as an example to the people of his church. He tried to build a name, not only for himself, but also for the God-given office of a pastor. This is why Mrs. Rasmussen often told her children, "You are a Rasmussen. Live up to that name. Don't do anything that would shame the name of Rasmussen."

God wants you to have His name. If you have not yet become a Christian, today can be your day of salvation! God wants to restore identity to you.

If you receive Jesus Christ into your heart, you are a Christian. You have a new name to represent. This name is above every name. Are you doing anything that would shame the name of Christ? Are you a holy Christian? You ought to be if you belong to God.

The next time you glance over the cover of your Bible, consider those two precious words engraved on the cover, "Holy Bible." The Bible is a holy Book because it is God's Book. When you choose to be God's child, you are called to a life of holiness because you belong to Him. Are you living a life yielded to His holiness? Are you holy as He is holy?

CHAPTER TWO

Revival God's Way

And on the three and twentieth day of the seventh month he sent the people away into their tents, glad and merry in heart for the goodness that the LORD had shewed unto David, and to Solomon, and to Israel his people. Thus Solomon finished the house of the LORD, and the king's house: and all that came into Solomon's heart to make in the house of the LORD, and in his own house, he prosperously effected. And the LORD appeared to Solomon by night, and said unto him, I have heard thy prayer, and have chosen this place to myself for an house of sacrifice. If I shut up heaven that there be no rain, or if I command the locusts to devour the land, or if I send pestilence among my people; If my people, which are called by

31

*my name, shall humble themselves, and pray, and seek
my face, and turn from their wicked ways; then will I
hear from heaven, and will forgive their sin, and will
heal their land.*—2 Chronicles 7:10–14

What is biblical revival? Is it a series of meetings hosted by a church? Is it an emphasis on prayer? Is revival just preaching or services? Can it be scheduled?

The 1857–1859 revival known as the Prayer Revival was the last time revival took place on American soil. It began on Fulton Street in New York City when six men met at the noon hour to pray. That noonday prayer meeting started to spread until the Old Dutch Reformed Church was too small to hold those who had come to pray. Other places were found where people met to pray, and soon the Prayer Meeting Revival began to spread across America and eventually across the Atlantic into England. By the time two years had ended, more than one million people were converted to Christ through the prayer meetings held at the noon hour each day.

I am not an expert on national revival. I have never personally experienced a national movement of God. I do not know what it is like to experience an awakening of God across the nation, but I have lived for, prayed for, and expected revival.

There is one pulpit in America from which I have preached more often than any other—the pulpit at

Camp Joy in Whitewater, Wisconsin. I have been preaching behind that pulpit once a year and sometimes multiple times a year for the last thirty years. Recently, I calculated preaching over eight hundred different sermons from that pulpit.

Dr. Charles Hatchett is the director of Camp Joy and has heard most of the messages I have preached at the camp. Recently, after preaching behind the camp pulpit, he walked up to me and said, "Brother Goetsch, every time I hear you speak, I sense this passion for revival. I sense that the expectation of revival is going to come. What gives you that expectation? What do you see in America tonight that causes you to expect revival?"

I thought for a moment and then I said, "Brother Hatchett, I don't see any evidence that we're going to have revival. In fact, I usually see just the opposite. But I don't have to see it to, by faith, believe that it can take place." The Bible says in Hebrews 11:1, *"Now faith is the substance of things hoped for, the evidence of things not seen."*

The Bible instructs us to walk by faith, not by sight. Regardless of what is happening outside the walls of your home or within fundamental independent churches, I believe we can see revival. Second Chronicles 7 gives us five ingredients for you and me to have biblical revival.

God Needs a Place

Although God is not limited to time and space, He needs a place to demonstrate His power! Second Chronicles 7:12 says, *"And the LORD appeared to Solomon by night, and said unto him, I have heard thy prayer, and have chosen this place to myself for an house of sacrifice."* Verse 15 says, *"Now mine eyes shall be open, and mine ears attent unto the prayer that is made in this place."*

The Temple That Solomon Built

In the Old Testament, God chose to demonstrate His power in the temple Solomon built. John 2:20 tells us, *"...Forty and six years was this temple in building...."* What a magnificent and amazing structure this temple was! If you were to study the building of the temple you would find that there was not one sound of a hammer, nor one sound of a saw at the temple. Every article that went into the temple was constructed offsite. When building articles were brought to Jerusalem to be constructed, not a sound was made and not a word was spoken out of a reverence to a holy God.

This temple was an amazing place. Just the gold inside was 108,000 talents. A talent was the largest measuring amount in the Jewish system. It was equivalent to the weight that an average man could carry, which is ninety-three pounds. Over one million pounds of gold was used on the inside alone. The temple, which displayed God's power, was a place of awe and beauty. It was a place of holiness.

In 2 Chronicles 7:1-5, the Bible says, *"Now when Solomon had made an end of praying, the fire came down from heaven, and consumed the burnt offering and the sacrifices; and the glory of the LORD filled the house. And the priests could not enter into the house of the LORD, because the glory of the LORD had filled the LORD's house. And when all the children of Israel saw how the fire came down, and the glory of the LORD upon the house, they bowed themselves with their faces to the ground upon the pavement, and worshipped, and praised the LORD, saying, For he is good; for his mercy endureth for ever. Then the king and all the people offered sacrifices before the LORD. And king Solomon offered a sacrifice of twenty and two thousand oxen, and an hundred and twenty thousand sheep: so the king and all the people dedicated the house of God."*

Wouldn't you have loved to attend the ceremony of dedication for the house of God? An amazing offering was made to the Lord in thanksgiving for what He had done for the people of Israel.

The Temple That Salvation Bought

While in the Old Testament, the temple built by Solomon was the place where God had chosen to demonstrate His power; in the New Testament, the place God chose to demonstrate His power was a temple bought by salvation. If you are saved, your body is the temple of the Holy Spirit! You are the place in which God wants to work! In 1 Corinthians 6:19, Paul says, *"What? know ye not that your body is the temple of the Holy Ghost which is in you, which ye have of God, and ye are not your own? For ye are bought with a price: therefore glorify God in your body, and in your spirit, which are God's."*

While the Old Testament temple was of great cost materially, the cost of salvation was even greater. The Old Testament builders gathered beautiful wood along with pure gold and silver to fashion and construct a temple. They offered many sacrifices in thanksgiving and praise for all God had done. Above the tremendous expense and cost that went into the temple, much more was paid for the gift of salvation. We were bought with a price so that we might be the temple of the living God—the dwelling place where God can work once again.

The psalmist David looked ahead to the crucifixion of Christ, to the price that would be paid to purchase our salvation. This prophecy is recorded in the Messianic Psalm 22:1–18, *"My God, my God, why hast thou forsaken me? why art thou so far from helping me, and from the words of my roaring? O my God, I cry in the daytime, but thou hearest not; and in the night season, and am not silent. But thou art holy, O thou that inhabitest the praises of Israel. Our fathers trusted in thee: they trusted, and thou didst deliver them. They cried unto thee, and were delivered: they trusted in thee, and were not confounded. But I am a worm, and no man; a reproach of men, and despised of the people. All they that see me laugh me to scorn: they shoot out the lip, they shake the head, saying, He trusted on the LORD that he would deliver him: let him deliver him, seeing he delighted in him. But thou art he that took me out of the womb: thou didst make me hope when I was upon my mother's breasts. I was cast upon thee from the womb: thou art my God from my mother's belly. Be not far from me; for trouble is near; for there is none to help. Many bulls have compassed me: strong bulls of Bashan have beset me round. They gaped upon me with their mouths, as a ravening and a roaring lion. I am poured out like water, and all my bones are out of joint: my heart is like wax; it is melted in the midst of my bowels. My strength is dried up like a potsherd; and my tongue cleaveth to my jaws; and thou hast brought me into the dust of death. For dogs have compassed me: the assembly of the wicked have inclosed me: they pierced my hands and my feet. I may tell all my bones: they look and stare upon me. They part my garments among them, and cast lots upon my vesture."*

This prophetic passage certainly portrays the great price that was paid for our salvation! Christ gave His back to the smiters, His cheeks to those who plucked off the hair; He hid not His face from shame. Jesus Christ, who purchased your temple, said in John 10:11, *"I am the good shepherd: the good shepherd giveth his life for the sheep."* Jesus paid the cost with His life.

God needs a place to dwell—a place to demonstrate His power. May He use your heart? He needs a place to show Himself strong; He needs a place to do miracles! Will you allow Him to find a home in your heart?

God Needs a Problem

God presented a hypothetical problem in 2 Chronicles 7:13, *"If I shut up heaven that there be no rain, or if I command the locusts to devour the land, or if I send pestilence among my people."* A revival is not mentioned in this passage of Scripture because there was no need for revival.

If you are reading this book, you do not need to be physically revived. You are obviously conscious, as you comprehend the contents of these paragraphs. But if suddenly you lost consciousness physically, you would have a problem—you would need revival. God is well aware of our human nature. He knew that Israel would lose perception of Him. He knew Israel would be prone to walk away from Him. He knew that man would stray. Because of His knowledge and understanding of human nature, God presents three parallels to a problem.

A Drought of Rain

Second Chronicles 7:13 states the first problem: "*If
I shut up heaven that there be no rain....*" Nothing is
more serious for an agricultural society like Israel than
a drought. Nothing could be more devastating to a
people, to a land, to an economy, or to social welfare
than a drought.

Nothing is more serious for God's people than a
spiritual drought! Isaiah 55:10–11 explains it this way,
"*For as the rain cometh down, and the snow from heaven,
and returneth not thither, but watereth the earth, and
maketh it bring forth and bud, that it may give seed to
the sower, and bread to the eater: So shall my word be
that goeth forth out of my mouth: it shall not return unto
me void, but it shall accomplish that which I please, and
it shall prosper in the thing whereto I sent it.*"

God parallels a drought of rain to a drought of
His Word. In Israel, during a season of drought, the
land was parched—there was no food, sustenance, nor
substance growing. When the Word of God is no longer
flowing in our lives, there is no substance and there is
no fruit of righteousness displayed in our lives.

Food grows where the water flows. Jesus said in
Matthew 22:29, "*...Ye do err, not knowing the scriptures,
nor the power of God.*" Jeremiah 8:9 says, "*The wise men
are ashamed, they are dismayed and taken: lo, they have
rejected the word of the LORD; and what wisdom is in*

them?" Outside the rain of God's Word, there is no wisdom. The world's knowledge is foolishness to God.

If we are getting answers for our spiritual problems from some place other than the Bible, we are getting the wrong answers. Proverbs 13:13 says, "*Whoso despiseth the word shall be destroyed.*" We must realize that "… *the word of God is quick, and powerful, and sharper than any twoedged sword, piercing even to the dividing asunder of soul and spirit, and of the joints and marrow, and is a discerner of the thoughts and intents of the heart*" (Hebrews 4:12). You may sing "Nothing Between My Soul and the Saviour" all day long and never realize there is something between you and your Saviour if you don't read your Bible.

Life may lead us down the road of complacency if we allow it, but the Word of God penetrates! The Word of God reveals. The Word of God uncovers and brings to light the very thoughts and intents of the heart. Jeremiah 17:9 says, "*The heart is deceitful above all things, and desperately wicked: who can know it?*"

Hosea 4:6 says, "*My people are destroyed for lack of knowledge: because thou hast rejected knowledge, I will also reject thee, that thou shalt be no priest to me: seeing thou hast forgotten the law of thy God, I will also forget thy children.*" My generation has decided that we don't need God anymore. We decided in the 1960s to take Him out of our schools. We took the Ten Commandments down from our hallways. We no longer could read the

Bible in our public education. Not only did we take the Bible out of our schools, we also took it out of our homes. There may still be one on the coffee table, but it is seldom opened. We have taken it out of our pulpits. Often people don't carry their Bibles to church—it is not needed because it is not used.

When we cling to human reasoning, experience, philosophy, our own ideas, and our own agendas, God says in Hosea 4:6, "...*seeing thou hast forgotten the law of thy God, I will also forget thy children.*" God will take away His hand of blessing and protection. The generation of today will not turn to God until the baby boomer generation of yesterday comes back to the Word of God. When we cease to have the rain of God's Word in our lives, we have a problem.

A Devouring of Righteousness

Second Chronicles 7:13 says, "...*if I command the locusts to devour the land.*" In this phrase, we find the second problem: a devouring of righteousness. The locusts of sin have been turned loose. Today in our nation, sin is promoted, and God is demoted. Folly is set in great dignity. Sin is not only protected today, it is preferred. Proverbs 15:21 says, "Folly is joy to him that is destitute of wisdom...."

Righteousness is being devoured by the locusts of sin. Proverbs 14:34 says, *"Righteousness exalteth a nation: but sin is a reproach to any people.*" I have yet to find a passage in all of the Bible that describes American culture better than Isaiah 59:12–15: "*For our transgressions are multiplied before thee, and our sins testify against us: for our transgressions are with us; and as for our iniquities, we know them; In transgressing and lying against the LORD, and departing away from our God, speaking oppression and revolt, conceiving and uttering from the heart words of falsehood. And judgment is turned away backward, and justice standeth afar off: for truth is fallen in the street, and equity cannot enter. Yea, truth faileth….*" The truth of our Lord is failing in our land because the locusts of sin are seeking to destroy and falsify righteousness.

A Damage of the Redeemed

The final phrase of 2 Chronicles 7:13 states, "*…or if I send pestilence among my people.*" Sin is not just affecting the culture, the unsaved corporate world, or the rebellious teenage lifestyles; sin is affecting God's people. We are seeing a damaging of the redeemed in our world today. Sin is affecting preachers, potential preachers, Christian homes, Christian school children, and Bible college students. The wolf does not prey on wolves; he preys on sheep. Jesus said in John 10:9–10, "*I am the door: by me if any man enter in, he shall be saved, and* *shall go in and out, and find pasture. The thief cometh not, but for to steal, and to kill, and to destroy...."*

God presented a hypothetical situation in 2 Chronicles 7. He saw past Israel's time of worship and dedication of the temple and knew even the redeemed would be facing a problem.

A pastor friend gave me a tape of an interview broadcast on the radio several years ago. It was an interview with a man who, at that time, was in his late eighties. This man was only fourteen years old when the Welsh revival broke loose.

During the Welsh revival, the meeting places became so filled that they would only allow adult men and any young men down to fourteen years of age to attend the meetings. There was no room for women and children. This man was only fourteen years old when he heard Ivan Roberts preach. Through this elderly man's Irish accent, I had to strain to hear exactly what he was saying as he talked about those services and how God began to sweep across the country of Wales. He spoke of the changes that began to take place because of that revival. I remember when the interviewer asked him a certain question. He said, "Sir, what was it like in Wales just before the revival?" I will never forget his answer, for it came so quickly. He said, "The people were as hard as flint." I remember listening to that tape in my car, and after hearing his response, I threw my hands in the air and exclaimed, "Hallelujah! We can have revival!"

Why? We are as hard as flint. Our problems can only be revived by the holy power of God.

God Needs a People

Revival Is Conditioned by an Awakened People

Second Chronicles 7:14 begins with three powerful words, *"If my people...."* The word *if* indicates circumstances that would have to exist in order for an event to happen. If—it is the one factor in revival that we don't know. The unanswered problem in the equation of revival is "If my people." Will God's people awaken? Will we who are saved awake to revival?

In Isaiah's day, his watchmen were blind. His watchmen were to be on guard, but instead they fell asleep—falling prey to the love of slumber. The church is also falling prey to sleep. Proverbs 10:5 says, *"He that gathereth in summer is a wise son: but he that sleepeth in harvest is a son that causeth shame."* Proverbs 6:9–11 says, *"How long wilt thou sleep, O sluggard? when wilt thou arise out of thy sleep? Yet a little sleep, a little slumber, a little folding of the hands to sleep: So shall thy poverty come as one that travelleth, and thy want as an armed man."*

America is sinking in spiritual poverty because God's people have not yet awakened. Romans 13:11 says, *"...now it is high time to awake out of sleep: for now is our salvation nearer than when we believed."* Wickedness and spiritual depravity are prevalent in our culture. We as Christians must awaken to God's call for revival! Let us put on the armor of light and redeem the time, because the days are evil.

Revival Is Chosen by an Attached People

Second Chronicles 7:14 says, *"If my people, which are called by my name...."* The key to revival is not found in governmental leaders or in Supreme Court justices. The key is not better laws or a better judicial system. The key to revival is found in the people who are called by God's name. God did not wait for Sodom to change; He waited for ten righteous people to step forward. God was well aware of what He could do at Nineveh, yet it took longer for God to get the preacher to Nineveh than it did for the entire city to repent! God needs people who are not only awakened, but people who are also attached to Him!

Matthew 5:13–14 reminds us of the importance of being an "attached" people: *"Ye are the salt of the earth: but if the salt have lost his savour, wherewith shall it be salted? it is thenceforth good for nothing, but to be cast out, and to be trodden under foot of men. Ye are the light of the world."* First Peter 2:9 motivates us to live righteously in a dark world: *"But ye are a chosen generation, a royal priesthood, an holy nation, a peculiar people; that ye should shew forth the praises of him who hath called you out of darkness into his marvellous light."* First Peter 2:11–12 compels us to walk with God and to walk as strangers in this world: *"Dearly beloved, I beseech you as strangers and pilgrims, abstain from fleshly lusts, which war against the soul; Having your conversation honest among the Gentiles: that, whereas they speak against you as evildoers, they may by your good works, which they shall behold, glorify God in the day of visitation."*

When I preach revival meetings, my heart is always blessed when I receive notes saying, "Brother Goetsch, I don't want to be the one who stands in the way." God is waiting for each one of us. Does revival tarry because of you? Will you be the one who stands in the way?

God Needs a Procedure

A Humble Contrition

Have you noticed that humility is a do-it-yourself project? Second Chronicles 7:14 continues to say, *"If my people...shall humble themselves...."* If we are waiting for God to humble us, humility will never come. God says in 1 Peter 5:6, *"Humble yourselves therefore under the mighty hand of God, that he may exalt you in due time."* It is not God's job to humble us; His job is to exalt us as we humble ourselves.

Micah 6:8 says, "...*what doth the* LORD *require of thee, but to do justly, and to love mercy, and to walk humbly with thy God?*" Peter said in 1 Peter 5:5 to be "...*clothed with humility....*" Why? Peter's answer comes in the same verse, "...*for God resisteth the proud, and giveth grace to the humble.*"

If we strut around and brag about our accomplishments, we will miss revival. Our selfish pride is destroying our homes, our nation, and ourselves. Pride is the root of it all. It is what destroyed Lucifer, and it is what will destroy us. According to Proverbs 16:18, "*Pride goeth before destruction, and an haughty spirit before a fall.*" Solomon said in Proverbs 21:4 that, "*An high look, and a proud heart, and the plowing of the wicked, is sin.*" Solomon left no room for question when he wisely stated Proverbs 16:5, "*Every one that is proud in heart is an abomination to the* LORD." No matter who you are—the evangelist, the preacher, the Sunday school teacher, or the custodian—every prideful heart is an abomination to the Lord.

A Heavenward Calling

God's procedure for revival requires humility, but it also requires prayer. We must call upon God according to 2 Chronicles 7:14, "*If my people...shall humble themselves, and pray....*" It is not the church that will bring revival. It is not the sermon, the evangelist, nor the program that will bring revival. Jeremiah 33:3 says, *"Call unto me, and I will answer thee, and shew thee great and mighty things, which thou knowest not."* Matthew 7:7 says, *"Ask, and it shall be given you; seek, and ye shall find; knock, and it shall be opened unto you:"* First John 5:14 says, *"And this is the confidence that we have in him, that, if we ask any thing according to his will, he heareth us."* James 5:16 says, *"The effectual fervent prayer of a righteous man availeth much."* Revival comes when God's people pray. Simple? Yes. Doable? Yes. You and I can be a part of a revival if we would just pray!

A Heartfelt Change

God's procedure for revival also calls for a heartfelt change. When we seek selfish desires, worldly acceptance, or other wrong things, revival cannot come. Second Chronicles 7:14 says, *"and seek my face…."* If God sent revival, would we seek Him or would we seek fame? I'm afraid if revival came, the first thing we would do is write a book about it. I fear we would go on television, give our testimonies, and tell the world how to obtain revival. We are seekers of fortune, success, and pleasure.

Many people come to church in search of happiness; few come to find holiness. Isaiah 55:6 says, *"Seek ye the LORD while he may be found, call ye upon him while he is near."* Jeremiah 29:13 says, *"And ye shall seek me, and find me, when ye shall search for me with all your heart."*

An Honest Confession

Second Chronicles 7:14 continues to outline God's procedure for revival: *"...and turn from their wicked ways...."* One of my pet peeves is how we sing the song, "Victory in Jesus." Whenever we sing this hymn, we sing it wrong! We do not pronounce one of the words correctly. The first verse begins, "I heard an old, old story, how a Saviour came from glory, how He gave His life on Calvary to save a wretch like me." Further on it says, "Then I repented of my sins and won the victory." It says sins, with an "s" instead of sin. The word *sin* is far too generic; the word *sins* is very specific. We can talk about sin all day long; we can discuss how much God hates sin. But which specific sins does He hate in your life and mine?

Have you ever heard the expression, "Those people are living in sin"? Why don't we refer to it as "sins"? God is waiting for His people to be honest about their sins. He is waiting for us to clean house because *"He that covereth his sins shall not prosper: but whoso confesseth and forsaketh them shall have mercy"* (Proverbs 28:13). We may say our house is clean, but God knows where the dirt is. *"Thou hast set our iniquities before thee, our secret sins in the light of thy countenance"* (Psalm 90:8).

Luke 12:2–3 says, *"For there is nothing covered, that shall not be revealed; neither hid, that shall not be known. Therefore whatsoever ye have spoken in darkness shall be heard in the light; and that which ye have spoken in the ear in closets shall be proclaimed upon the housetops."* Hebrews 4:13 says, *"Neither is there any creature that is not manifest in his sight: but all things are naked and opened unto the eyes of him with whom we have to do."*

When you and I honestly confess sins with a broken heart and willing spirit, God will not forsake us; rather, He will help us. Psalm 51:17, reminds us that *"…a broken and a contrite heart, O God, thou wilt not despise."*

God Gives a Promise

Not only does God provide a procedure in 2 Chronicles 7:14, He further reveals a promise,, *"…then will I hear from heaven, and will forgive their sin, and will heal their land."* When we, as God's people, follow God's procedure concerning the problem we see in a place called our hearts, then God gives us a promise!

The Promise of a Hearing Ear

Second Chronicles 7:14 says, *"…then will I hear from heaven…."* Has God heard our prayer for revival? God promises us His hearing ear. Psalm 34:15 promises, *"The eyes of the LORD are upon the righteous, and his ears are open unto their cry.*" Isaiah 65:24 states, *"And it shall come to pass, that before they call, I will answer; and while they are yet speaking, I will hear."* If we want God to hear our prayers for revival, we must willingly remove from our lives that which is wrong and sinful. The Lord hears the cries of the righteous. He is willing to do something beyond our expectations, but we must be willing to do what it takes to have God hear our prayers.

The Promise of a Holy Eradication

Second Chronicles 7:14 continues, *"I will forgive their sin...."* God promises His forgiveness! His Word says in 1 John 1:9, *"If we confess our sins, he is faithful and just to forgive us our sins, and to cleanse us from all unrighteousness."* I'm glad the word *all* is in this verse. We have sin in our lives that makes God sick—pride, selfishness, bitterness, jealousy, envy—and these are often the sins about which no one knows. But God is able to forgive all of them! Psalm 103:12 says, *"As far as the east is from the west, so far hath he removed our transgressions from us."* God proclaimed in Isaiah 43:25, *"I, even I, am he that blotteth out thy transgressions for mine own sake, and will not remember thy sins."*

God wants to forgive us far more than we want to be forgiven. God wants a clean house, a purified people, a vessel of honor sanctified for the Master's use.

God wants a holy eradication, and He delights in the process.

Micah said in Micah 7:18, "...*he retaineth not his anger for ever, because he delighteth in mercy.*" God delights in mercy. Like the father of the prodigal son who waited and longed for his son to come home, God waits and lingers at the doors of our hearts hoping that they would open to Him again. He longs for us to bend our knees before Him, and cry out to Him in our shame and repentance, and say, "I'm tired of my sins; I'm tired of my wickedness. Lord, I come back to You." This is when the Father rejoices, for He delights in mercy. "*...Bring forth the best robe, and put it on him; and put a ring on his hand, and shoes on his feet: And bring hither the fatted calf, and kill it; and let us eat, and be merry*" (Luke 15:22–23).

The Promise of a Healing Experience

Second Chronicles 7:14 ends, "*I will heal their land.*" Our nation can be restored! We can hope in God's promise of healing our land.

Many years ago, a university in the state of Michigan set out to find the kindest city in America. They sent college students to every major city in America. These students pretended to be blind, old, and in need of help. They faked a broken car, they faked running out of gas; they wanted to see where in America most people would be kind to them.

They not only did this once; they did it twice, fifty years apart. Amazingly, the results were the same. They found the kindest city in America to be Rochester, New York. They published their survey results.

A newspaperman in New York City couldn't believe what he had read. He lived in New York. He imagined a city in the south would rank highest due to their southern hospitality, or a western city with their open-mindedness. But Rochester, New York? That reporter, according to *Readers' Digest*, traveled to Rochester to find out why. The man began to observe and inquire. He found that Rochester was the only city in America that had its own health care system. He found orphanages, well-equipped prisons, and homeless shelters. He began to realize that the survey was no doubt true. But while he acknowledged it, he wanted to find out why. He began to trace the city's history. Documentation traced Rochester's history back to a revival in which Evangelist Finney preached, and 100,000 people were converted in Rochester, New York.

I don't know if anyone will conduct a survey like that one fifty years from now. I don't know if people will be searching for the place where revival started. But I know this: God is looking for a place. If someone were to search for the genesis of revival fifty years from now, would they be able to trace it to your heart?

CHAPTER THREE

The Barrier to Revival

Do you believe God can send revival? Do you think He has lost the power or desire to send revival? The Bible says in Psalm 62:11, "*God hath spoken once; twice have I heard this; that power belongeth unto God.*" God has always had the power to do anything He desires to do. In Job 42:2 the Bible says, "*I know that thou canst do every thing, and that no thought can be withholden from thee.*" Ephesians 3:20 says, "*Now unto him that is able to do exceeding abundantly above all that we ask or think, according to the power that worketh in us.*" God has the power to give revival because "*…with God nothing shall be impossible*" (Luke 1:37).

Have we considered that perhaps *we* are the very barriers to revival? D.L. Moody once said, "The man I fear the most is the one who walks underneath this hat." Do we fear standing in the way of revival? The problem must be with us because revival is not being hindered by God.

Every morning, I get into my car and drive to work, church, or a meeting. The car belongs to me, and it is paid for in full. I have the title. The registration is in the glove box. There is gas in the tank, and the license plates are up-to-date. It is legally *my* car. But if I gave my keys to you, I wouldn't be able to go anywhere. It is still my car. I own it and put gas in it. I paid for the insurance, registration, and license. But without the key, I'm left to another resort—walking!

This is God's universe. He owns it and created it. We are His creation. As children of God, the Holy Spirit lives within us—giving us access to the power of God. We have the promises in the Bible of His power, His protection, and His provision, but we hold the key. God purchased us with the blood of Jesus, but He does not have the key to all of our lives, because some of us are still hanging on to our "keys."

God is able to do something we cannot comprehend. But the unanswered question is *"If my people…."* Are we going to turn the key over to God? Are we going to remove that barrier from our lives and let God have His way? That is the question. The questions are not, "God, are You going to send revival? God, when are *You* going to work? God, when are we going to see something great happen?" The question is whether or not *we* are going to give God the key.

What in our lives is hindering God's power? What is the barrier keeping God from sending revival to you and me? James 4 reveals keys to our hearts that serve as barriers to revival.

A Problem Discovered

A Contentious Paradigm

The first problem in the barrier to revival is a contentious paradigm. James 4:1 says, "*From whence come wars and fightings among you? come they not hence , even of your lusts that war in your members?*" The devil loves strife; he loves to disturb things on the ground level of God's work.

As I have traveled this country preaching in many churches over the past several years, I have seen very few churches split over doctrinal issues. But, I have seen many churches split.

In Acts 2:47, "*…the Lord added to the church daily such as should be saved.*" God used a mathematical term—He added. In Acts 12:24, "*…the word of God grew and multiplied.*" He used another mathematical term—He multiplied. (Although I was not a math major, I do know this much: you can get to a place faster by multiplying than you can by adding! Two plus three is five, but two multiplied by three is six.) God began to bless the early church. In the early days, God was adding to the church daily. Later, God was multiplying the work.

Even if God wants to add to the church and send revival today, He cannot do so if we are subtracting, and He cannot multiply if we are dividing. Matthew 5:23–24 says, "*Therefore if thou bring thy gift to the altar, and there rememberest that thy brother hath ought against thee; Leave there thy gift before the altar, and go thy way; first be reconciled to thy brother, and then come and offer thy gift.*" God is not interested in revival meetings if we are not right with one another. We must be right with each other before we can experience revival. This is what God requires of us. We will not go anywhere until God holds the keys in this area.

I have heard people pray, "Lord, where two or three are gathered together, thank You, Lord, that You're in the midst." Did you know God never said that? "Well, if we pray in Jesus' name, He's there." No, He didn't say that either.

Matthew 18:15–20 says, "*Moreover if thy brother shall trespass against thee, go and tell him his fault between thee and him alone: if he shall hear thee, thou hast gained thy brother. But if he will not hear thee, then take with thee one or two more, that in the mouth of two or three witnesses every word may be established. And if he shall neglect to hear them, tell it unto the church: but if he neglect to hear the church, let him be unto thee as an heathen man and a publican. Verily I say unto you, Whatsoever ye shall bind on earth shall be bound in heaven: and whatsoever ye shall loose on earth shall be loosed in heaven. Again I say unto you, That if two of you shall agree on earth as touching any thing that they shall ask, it shall be done for them of my Father which is in heaven. For where two or three are gathered together in my name, there am I in the midst of them."*

If I were to walk up to you and say, "Look at those shoes! I have never seen shoes so ugly in my life. You must have paid way too much money at a thrift store for those!" You may respond, "Hey, I love these shoes! They are my most comfortable pair. My grandmother bought me these shoes, and I will wear them if I want!"

Now, if I continued to make fun of you because of your hideous shoes, and you started getting angry with me, this situation is bound in Heaven because it is bound on earth.

Let's say I begin to feel convicted for making fun of you, so I approach you and apologize. After hearing my apology, you begin to confess that you were mad and may not have reacted as you should have. Our relationship is now made right. It has been loosed on earth.

This illustration explains what Matthew was saying. What is loosed on earth is also loosed in Heaven, and now God can be present because two people agree. Matthew was not talking about agreeing to pray; he was talking about being in agreement so we can pray. Our relationships must be in agreement for God to be with us when we pray.

Is there someone with whom you are not right? Are you in agreement with all of your family members? Is there someone with whom you cannot speak or even give a smile? Who don't you want to run into at church? Ephesians 4:30–32 says, "*...grieve not the holy Spirit of God, whereby ye are sealed unto the day of redemption. Let all bitterness, and wrath, and anger, and clamour, and evil speaking, be put away from you, with all malice: And be ye kind one to another, tenderhearted, forgiving one another, even as God for Christ's sake hath forgiven you.*" You may think, "You don't know what they did to me. You just don't understand." True. I may not understand. But if God can forgive me for all my sins, there is nobody I cannot forgive. And if God can forgive you for all of your sins, there should be nobody you cannot forgive. James 5:16 says, "*Confess your faults one to another....*" Paul says in Acts 24:16, "*And herein do I exercise myself, to have always a conscience void of offence toward God, and toward men.*" Proverbs 16:7 says, "*When a man's ways please the LORD, he maketh even his enemies to be at peace with him.*"

A Canceled Prayer Life

James 4:2 says, "*Ye lust, and have not: ye kill, and desire to have, and cannot obtain: ye fight and war, yet ye have not, because ye ask not.*" Herein lies the second barrier to revival: a canceled prayer life. When your fellowship with man is marred, it is obvious that your fellowship with God stopped a long time before your trouble with earthly relationships. When we do not get along with one another, it is often because we are not right with God.

Cain's problem was not with Abel. Cain's problem was with God. Because God is a Spirit, Cain could only take his frustration or anger out on Abel; and thus, he murdered him.

Jesus reminds us that when we are not right with one another, it is because we have first cut off communication with God—there has been a canceled prayer life. Zephaniah 1:6 says, "*And them that are turned back from the LORD; and those that have not sought the LORD, nor enquired for him.*" Someone who has turned away from God and the things of the Lord is someone who has first abandoned his prayer life. It should not surprise us that someone would turn away from God if he isn't praying, because every relationship is marred by a lack of communication. You can't sustain a good relationship if you don't talk. When we stop communicating with God, is it any wonder that we walk away from Him? Is it any wonder that we are holding on to the key that is keeping us from revival?

A Covetous Pursuit

James 4:3 continues to list barriers to revival: "*Ye ask, and receive not, because ye ask amiss, that ye may consume it upon your lusts.*" What on your prayer list would be important one hundred years from now? What are you praying for that is going to matter for eternity? When we come into the presence of God in prayer, we tend to pray selfishly. Our prayers often reveal a covetous pursuit.

A couple of weeks before Christmas, our granddaughters were visiting for a couple days. I was walking by the kitchen counter, and my four-year-old granddaughter had a catalog open. She had a pen in one hand, and she was turning pages with the other hand. Every time she turned a page, she would circle five items. I said, "Katie, what are you doing?" She looked up at me and said, "I'm circling what I'm getting for Christmas." I said, "All of those things?" She said, "Whatever I circle, I get."

Sometimes I wonder if God sees our prayer list in the same way I looked at Katie's Christmas list. He sees how we circle the things we selfishly desire—the things we want God to do for us rather than praying according to His will. First John 5:14 says, "*And this is the confidence that we have in him, that, if we ask any thing according to his will, he heareth us."* Psalm 40:8 says, *"I delight to do thy will, O my God: yea, thy law is within my heart."* Are we covetously circling what we want, or are we delightfully asking according to His will?

A Carnal Passion

James 4:4 says, *"Ye adulterers and adulteresses, know ye not that the friendship of the world is enmity with God? whosoever therefore will be a friend of the world is the enemy of God."* Nothing will keep you from the pursuit of God more than the pursuit of your flesh. As the bride of Christ, Christians cannot expect the blessings of God in revival when they are in bed with the world. This is what James is referring to when he says, *"Ye adulterers and adulteresses...."* The Bridegroom is about to split the eastern sky! He is about to come and take His bride to the marriage supper of the Lamb. But when He comes, will He find His bride in bed with the world? Will He find Christians involved in carnal passions?

You may say, "This is the twenty-first century. There are so many temptations around, it is impossible to resist them all." Titus 2:12 says, *"Teaching us that, denying ungodliness and worldly lusts, we should live soberly, righteously, and godly, in this present world;"* We live in a wicked day, but God said, "...*in this present world.*" God knew what we would face in the twenty-first century. He already knew about the Internet, the radio, the Hollywood movies, and the video games—but knowing of all these temptations, He still wants us to live righteously and godly in this present world.

Second Corinthians 6:14–18 says, "*Be ye not unequally yoked together with unbelievers: for what fellowship hath righteousness with unrighteousness? and what communion hath light with darkness? And what concord hath Christ with Belial? or what part hath he that believeth with an infidel? And what agreement hath the temple of God with idols? for ye are the temple of the living God; as God hath said, I will dwell in them, and walk in them; and I will be their God, and they shall be my people. Wherefore come out from among them, and be ye separate, saith the Lord, and touch not the unclean thing; and I will receive you, And will be a Father unto you, and ye shall be my sons and daughters, saith the Lord Almighty.*" God is ready to work in our lives, but we must get rid of the carnal, fleshly, worldly passions that are driving us. First John 2:15–17 says, "*Love not the world, neither the things that are in the world. If any man love the world, the love of the Father is not in him. For all that is in the world, the lust of the flesh, and the lust of the eyes, and the pride of life, is not of the Father, but is of the world. And the world passeth away, and the lust thereof: but he that doeth the will of God abideth for ever.*"

A Process Defined

James has established a definite problem—beginning with you and me. James goes on to discuss defining a process. We all realize our need for revival, and we know we are the problem hindering its coming. So how do we fix it? How do we get to the place where God can work in our lives?

A Requirement of Submission

In James 4:6–7, we find the first step in God's refining process: submission. The Bible says, "*But he giveth more grace. Wherefore he saith, God resisteth the proud, but giveth grace unto the humble. Submit yourselves therefore to God….*" Humble yourselves. How do we fix the problem? How do we get to the place where God can once again give us revival? It starts with submission. Proverbs 6:16 tells us, "*These six things doth the LORD hate: yea, seven are an abomination unto him: A proud look….*" Submit to God; humble yourself.

There are examples in the Bible when people refused to submit and refused to humble themselves. There once lived an Old Testament king by the name of Nebuchadnezzar. Daniel, speaking to Nebuchadnezzar's grandson in Daniel 5:18–19 says, "*O thou king, the most high God gave Nebuchadnezzar thy father a kingdom, and majesty, and glory, and honour: And for the majesty that he gave him, all people, nations, and languages, trembled and feared before him: whom he would he slew; and whom he would he kept alive; and whom he would he set up; and whom he would he put down."* Here was Nebuchadnezzar, perhaps the most powerful king the world had ever seen. When his name was mentioned, people trembled. When he commanded a man to be put to death, the man was killed with no questions asked.

Daniel 5:20–21 continues to say, *"But when his heart was lifted up, and his mind hardened in pride, he was deposed from his kingly throne, and they took his glory from him: And he was driven from the sons of men; and his heart was made like the beasts, and his dwelling was with the wild asses: they fed him with grass like oxen, and his body was wet with the dew of heaven…."* The most powerful king in the world was sent out into the field kingdomless, familyless, and powerless. He was abased—eating grass like the oxen and finding a home among the asses. Because of his pride and lack of submission to God, God taught him humility.

There lived another king in the New Testament age by the name of Herod. The downfall of his life is recorded in Acts 12:21–23, *"And upon a set day Herod, arrayed in royal apparel, sat upon his throne, and made an oration unto them. And the people gave a shout, saying, It is the voice of a god, and not of a man. And immediately the angel of the Lord smote him, because he gave not God the glory: and he was eaten of worms, and gave up the ghost."*

He was killed simply because He did not give God the glory. Is there anything in your life for which you are not giving God the glory? What about your talents, your job, your health, your family? The Scripture says, "*...he was eaten of worms, and gave up the ghost.*" He did not die first and then the worms ate him; the worms ate him, then he died. God hates pride. He requires us to humble ourselves, so that He may exalt us in due time and receive the glory for what He accomplishes through our lives.

A Resistance of Satan

In addition to submission, God requires the resistance of Satan in our daily refining process. James 4:7 says, "*Submit yourselves therefore to God. Resist the devil, and he will flee from you.*" Satan is our enemy. We are battling in a spiritual warfare against him. This battle is not against flesh and blood. The battle is against spiritual wickedness in high places. Do you realize who your enemy is? Do you know of his power? John 8:44 says, "*Ye are of your father the devil, and the lusts of your father ye will do. He was a murderer from the beginning, and abode not in the truth, because there is no truth in him. When he speaketh a lie, he speaketh of his own: for he is a liar, and the father of it.*"

The devil has never one time spoken the truth. Everything he uses to tempt us is a lie. Yet we invite him into our lives. We invite him into our homes. We invite him into our entertainment systems; and we invite him into our computers and into our minds. He is our enemy, so *"Be sober, be vigilant; because your adversary the devil, as a roaring lion, walketh about, seeking whom he may devour"* (1 Peter 5:8). He is not trying to wound you; he is trying to kill you. His goal is to destroy you. He does not simply want to hinder you from being effective for God; he wants to ruin all of the influence you exert for God! He wants to waste your life, and that is why Proverbs 1:10 says, *"My son, if sinners entice thee, consent thou not."*

A Restoring of Sequence

James 4:8 says, *"Draw nigh to God, and he will draw nigh to you…."* Would you like to be closer to God? It is your move. You may be waiting for God to do something, but you must make the first move. When you find yourself in trouble or having messed up, God will help. But you must first draw near to Him, before He will respond and draw near to you. He will move when you move.

After an evening service, a man approached me and introduced himself. Because I had just used a football illustration in my sermon the night before, he said, "I used to play football."

"You did?" I asked. This gentleman was older in age and short in stature. I could sense that he wanted to talk about it, so I continued, "Well, did you play in high school?"

"Yeah. I wasn't on the team until my sophomore year. The coach said I was pretty good. In fact, the coach said that if I stuck with it, I'd probably be the best running back the school had ever seen. During my sophomore year, they made me a running back, and the first ten times I touched the ball, nobody touched me."

"Really?" I asked, knowing what a hard feat that would be. "You mean the first ten times you actually touched the ball, you scored and nobody could even touch you?"

He said, "Oh, I was very quick. I'd give them that move, and I was gone." His face began to show discouragement as he said, "I never played out my sophomore year."

"What happened? Did you get hurt?"

"No," he said, "I flunked geometry. My mind couldn't figure out those abstract formulas, and I just couldn't get it. I know I should have asked the teacher for help, but I was a shy kid."

I really didn't know how to respond to him. He was in his fifties and still thinking about it to this day. All he had to do was make a move. All he had to do was take the first step and ask for help, but he didn't.

"I know the teacher would have helped me. I was just bashful and ashamed that I couldn't get it," he said.

I thought to myself, this guy might have been in the Hall of Fame today, but he didn't make a move. He didn't draw nigh to the teacher. The teacher would have drawn nigh to him had he made a move. The teacher would have helped him and explained concepts to him. But you see, he was afraid to make the first move.

I am convinced there is great potential for revival that could be read in history books to come, but I wonder if we are going to make that move. We must restore the sequence. Here we are, waiting on God and saying, "God, do something! Work in our church! Save more people! Give us money for the buildings!" We are waiting for God to make a move, but God has placed that choice in our court. It is our move. We must draw nigh first. I wonder what God would do if all the Christians in America would take a step toward God. We have learned that we are the barrier to revival, and we now know how to fix it—draw nigh to Him!

A Repentance of Sin

James 4:8 says, "*Draw nigh to God, and he will draw nigh to you. Cleanse your hands, ye sinners....*" God wants us to cleanse our hands of any sin—to repent. First Corinthians 15:34 says, "*Awake to righteousness, and sin not...."* When God mentions repentance, it usually refers to salvation, but the Bible also mentions it in the matter of the Christian life. Acts 8:22 says, *"Repent therefore of this thy wickedness, and pray God, if perhaps the thought of thine heart may be forgiven thee."* We have become so afraid of this word *repentance* that we rarely mention it; but the truth is, we need repentance. We need to turn our backs on our old ways and our old wickedness. We need to confess and forsake our sins. We need to stop making excuses, stop rationalizing, stop blaming others, and repent.

A Renewing of Singleness

James 4:8 continues with God's process for experiencing revival, *"Draw nigh to God, and he will draw nigh to you. Cleanse your hands, ye sinners; and purify your hearts, ye double minded."* Do you find yourself wanting to serve two masters? Do you pray for revival but still desire to live in Egypt? God is calling Christians to singleness of heart.

Too often, Christians want the blessings of God with the benefits of the world, but God says in Matthew 6:24, *"No man can serve two masters: for either he will hate the one, and love the other; or else he will hold to the one, and despise the other. Ye cannot serve God and mammon."* First Corinthians 10:21 declares, *"Ye cannot drink the cup of the Lord, and the cup of devils: ye cannot*

be partakers of the Lord's table, and of the table of devils."
We cannot see revival if we are hanging on to the things
of the world.

In Joshua 24:15, Joshua said, *"And if it seem evil
unto you to serve the LORD, choose you this day whom
ye will serve; whether the gods which your fathers served
that were on the other side of the flood, or the gods of the
Amorites, in whose land ye dwell: but as for me and my
house, we will serve the LORD."*

At the top of Mount Carmel, Elijah told the people
in 1 Kings 18:21, *"How long halt ye between two opinions?
if the LORD be God, follow him: but if Baal, then follow
him. And the people answered him not a word."* I believe
one of the saddest verses in all the Bible is found in
1 Kings 18:21, *"...And the people answered him not a
word."*

There was a contest between the prophets of Baal
and the prophet of God. The people wanted to see who
could call down fire from Heaven. Before the contest
started, Elijah made a plea for the people to choose
whose side they were on, but the people remained
silent, unable to make a choice. They may have been
holding out, wondering if Elijah's God was really going
to win over Baal. Many people want to serve the true
God, but they are holding out—wondering if God can
really send revival. James 1:8 says, *"A double minded
man is unstable in all his ways."* We need a renewing of

singleness, *"…not with eyeservice, as menpleasers; but in singleness of heart, fearing God"* (Colossians 3:22).

A Revival of Sobriety

We need a revival of sobriety. James 4:9 says, *"Be afflicted, and mourn, and weep: let your laughter be turned to mourning, and your joy to heaviness."* Revival is not a party; neither is church for entertainment. People want to be happy, but sadly, not many want to be holy. True joy will come when people choose holiness over happiness. There is joy in serving Christ, and there is joy in getting completely right with God. The journey of holiness produces pure joy.

A Realignment of Success

James 4:10 says, *"Humble yourself in the sight of the Lord, and he shall lift you up."* This world's view of success is wrong. Everybody is trying to climb the ladder of success, pushing off anyone who stands in their way as they go up. They are trying to find the highest rung of the ladder, no matter what the cost—no ethics, no morals, no concern for others.

Philippians 2:5–7 says, *"Let this mind be in you, which was also in Christ Jesus: Who, being in the form of God, thought it not robbery to be equal with God: But made himself of no reputation, and took upon him the form of a servant, and was made in the likeness of men."*

Could you implement this verse into your resume? If someone were to ask you what you have been doing for the last ten years, could you reply, "Making myself of no reputation"? This is not the way the world thinks, is it? But Jesus worked to make Himself of no reputation, and He took upon Him the form of a servant.

My job is to train Bible college students through the ministry of West Coast Baptist College. Oftentimes, I challenge the college students to go out into their new areas of ministry, summer ministry or weekend ministry, and find the lowest rung of the ladder. I tell them to find the job that nobody else wants and to serve there! Nobody will be fighting for that position, but that is alright. Nobody may notice, but God notices. One day, God will turn the ladder around. Luke 14:11 says, *"For whosoever exalteth himself shall be abased; and he that humbleth himself shall be exalted."* We need to realign our thinking with God's thinking on success. Mark 10:45 says, *"For even the Son of man came not to be ministered unto, but to minister, and to give his life a ransom for many."*

A Restraining of Speech

James 4:11–12 says, *"Speak not evil one of another, brethren. He that speaketh evil of his brother, and judgeth his brother, speaketh evil of the law, and judgeth the law: but if thou judge the law, thou art not a doer of the law, but a judge. There is one lawgiver, who is able to save and to destroy: who art thou that judgest another?"* We need to learn to restrain our speech.

I realize I live a sheltered life. I spend the majority of my time at West Coast Baptist College working alongside some of the godliest people I know. I recognize that it is a privilege and that some people would give anything to work in a Christian environment because it is not easy working in the world. Although I do not get out in the world like many others, allow me to be honest. I hear God's name taken in vain more in churches across the country than anywhere else. Paul said in 1 Timothy 6:3, *"If any man teach otherwise, and consent not to wholesome words, even the words of our Lord Jesus Christ, and to the doctrine which is according to godliness; He is proud, knowing nothing…."*

If Jesus Christ in the flesh walked into the back door of your church, do you think He would take God's name in vain? He would not, so why would we? We are going to give an account for every word. Jesus said in Matthew 12:36–37, *"That every idle word that men shall speak, they shall give account thereof in the day of judgment. For by thy words thou shalt be justified, and by thy words thou shalt be condemned."* The psalmist prayed in Psalm 19:14, *"Let the words of my mouth, and the meditation of my heart, be acceptable in thy sight, O Lord, my strength, and my redeemer."*

A Prideful Delay

A Confident Security

James 4:13 portrays a confident security that causes a delay in experiencing true revival: "*Go to now, ye that say, To day or to morrow we will go into such a city, and continue there a year, and buy and sell, and get gain.*" We read books and hear about people getting saved, experiencing revival and taking the necessary steps to get right with God. We know we should do all of these, but we shrug and say, "Well, there's time."

Recently in a meeting I attended, the discussion led to people with addictions. Someone mentioned the term "functioning addict." In other words, this would be someone who had an addiction but could function in life like normal. They may be addicted to alcohol, drugs, pornography, or something of this nature, but they are still respected in the community. They are still able to hold down their jobs. Their marriages are intact, and their families are together.

I believe the church is full of "functioning sinners." They are addicted to secret sin, but their sin has not caught up with them yet. There may be Christians who still teach a class, still sing in the choir, still teach in the Christian school, still attend Bible college; but they are functioning sinners. First Corinthians 15:32 says, "*...let us eat and drink; for to* *morrow we die."* Acts 24:25 says, *"...Go thy way for this time; when I have a convenient season, I will call for thee."* The problem is, when you are ready to call on God, He may not answer. It may be too late.

A Cautioning Sermon

James 4:14–15 says, *"Whereas ye know not what shall be on the morrow. For what is your life? It is even a vapour, that appeareth for a little time, and then vanisheth away. For that ye ought to say, If the Lord will, we shall live, and do this, or that."* In this passage, God reminds us that we have no guarantee of time. David said in 1 Samuel 20:3, *"...there is but a step between me and death."* First Peter 1:24 says, *"For all flesh is as grass, and all the glory of man as the flower of grass. The grass withereth, and the flower thereof falleth away."* Job 14:2 says, *"He cometh forth like a flower, and is cut down: he fleeth also as a shadow, and continueth not."* Hebrews 9:27 says, *"And as it is appointed unto men once to die...."* You and I have an appointment with death. We all have a death day, just as sure as we have a birthday.

Have you ever said, "I'll make that decision later"? God is cautioning you regarding the uncertainty of your time on earth. Are you living in the now? Are you right with God today? There is no promise of tomorrow. You must allow God to change you today!

A Conscious Stubbornness

James 4:16, "*But now ye rejoice in your boastings: all such rejoicing is evil.*" Jeremiah 8:7 says, "*Yea, the stork in the heaven knoweth her appointed times; and the turtle and the crane and the swallow observe the time of their coming; but my people know not the judgment of the LORD.*" All of God's creation knows the times and the seasons. The birds know when to fly south; they know when to come back to the north. The animals know when to hibernate; they know when to gather food and when to store it. All God's creatures know that there are appointed times, but God's people cannot figure out the importance of the day they are going to die and meet the Lord.

A Condemning Sin

James 4:17 says, "*Therefore to him that knoweth to do good, and doeth it not, to him it is sin.*" You and I are responsible for the truth we know. I used to preach a message entitled "The Sin of Knowing Your Bible." I would start the message by saying, "Could it be a sin to know your Bible?" And the answer is, "Yes." If you are saved and you know it is right to be baptized, but you decide to wait, it is sin. If you know you ought to tithe according to the Bible, and you keep your money from the Lord, it is sin. If you know you ought to get right with your spouse, and you don't do it, it is sin. The ball is in your court. The key is in your hands.

During the revival in Wales in the early 1900s, a London newspaper was intrigued by the stories coming out of Wales of a great revival. The London newspaper wanted to get the story, so they sent their two best reporters to Wales. These reporters arrived in Wales and began to look around, searching for the churches and the auditoriums where the preaching was, but as they continued to search, they kept coming up empty. They couldn't find where these meetings were taking place, so finally in their haste to get the story and the report back, they walked up to a policeman standing on the corner and asked, "Sir, can you please tell us where the Welsh revival is taking place?" The policeman smiled and said, "Yes, I can. The revival is taking place underneath this uniform." Friend, that is where revival needs to take place—underneath this uniform—and we hold the key.

The minute we give the key back to God, the engine will start. The process of God sweeping once again with His mighty power across this land will begin. Let's not hang onto the key. It belongs to God anyway. It is His universe, and we are His creatures. God has His blessings ready to give. He has everything in place for revival, but we have to turn over the key.

CHAPTER FOUR

The Breath of Revival

Physically, revival is a restoring of breath. If someone were to pass out or lose consciousness, perhaps a firefighter or an EMT would come to him and help him to breathe again—he would need to be revived. Breathing is normal; not breathing is not normal. When you breathe, you are taking air in and exhaling it out—this is called respiration. But in reality, it's not really just air that you are breathing in and out. There is a difference between the air that is inhaled and the air that is exhaled. We say we're breathing air, but in reality, we're breathing air that contains oxygen. We're exhaling carbon dioxide. If someone were to lose consciousness, in order to be revived, the respiration process would need to be restored, that is, inhaling the oxygen and exhaling the carbon dioxide.

Revival relates with the human body just as much as it does with the spiritual body. Many Christians are unconscious to God's Word, and they need to be revived—to wake up to God's pleading call on their lives. Christians need to catch the breath of spiritual normalcy—the breath of revival.

God can and wants to restore our breathing. He wants us to breathe in and out, taking deep breaths as we go. He wants us to breathe in naturally—with oxygen— and breathe out naturally—with carbon dioxide. We are not supposed to breathe in and out the same thing—this would be abnormal breathing.

We are to breathe in the freshness of God's Word, and breathe out the harmfulness of sin. If we breathe in God's Word and breathe out God's Word, what good will this do our bodies? If our bodies breathed oxygen in and out, we would not retain the oxygen needed to stay alive; therefore, we would have need for another revival!

The bottom line of spiritual revival is getting back to normal breathing—getting the carbon dioxide out of our lives and the oxygen into our lives. The problem is that some Christians have lost consciousness, and they have lost their pattern for normal breathing. Some have been too busy inhaling all of the good works, but forgetting to exhale their secret sins, causing their spiritual bodies to lose consciousness.

We need to get back to the healthy breathing process. I'm afraid we come to church and get under conviction about the carbon dioxide in our lives, and by God's grace come to the altar to rid our lives of what it is that's wrong. But what can happen, in this world filled with carbon dioxide, is that we go back into our workplaces, into our schools, or into our homes and breathe carbon dioxide back in to our lives.

Guess what? This isn't normal breathing! You won't last long. Breathing in carbon dioxide and exhaling it out, then breathing it back in will kill you. You can't function humanly and normally this way. There needs to be a balance between carbon dioxide and oxygen.

If all we do is get our heads inside the canopy of revival, and all we do is breathe carbon dioxide back in when we go home, we are not going to be any different. We are going to be dead. We are not going to be alive, functional, or someone God can use. We must breathe in oxygen and breathe out the carbon dioxide.

Titus 2:1–15 says, "*But speak thou the things which become sound doctrine: That the aged men be sober, grave, temperate, sound in faith, in charity, in patience. The aged women likewise, that they be in behaviour as becometh holiness, not false accusers, not given to much wine; teachers of good things; That they may teach the young women to be sober, to love their husbands, to love their children, To be discreet, chaste, keepers at home, good, obedient to their own husbands, that the word of*

God be not blasphemed. Young men likewise exhort to be sober minded. In all things shewing thyself a pattern of good works: in doctrine shewing uncorruptness, gravity, sincerity, Sound speech, that cannot be condemned, that he that is of the contrary part may be ashamed, having no evil thing to say of you. Exhort servants to be obedient unto their own masters, and to please them well in all things; not answering again; Not purloining, but shewing all good fidelity; that they may adorn the doctrine of God our Saviour in all things. For the grace of God that bringeth salvation hath appeared to all men, Teaching us that, denying ungodliness and worldly lusts, we should live soberly, righteously, and godly, in this present world; Looking for that blessed hope, and the glorious appearing of the great God and our Saviour Jesus Christ; Who gave himself for us, that he might redeem us from all iniquity, and purify unto himself a peculiar people, zealous of good works. These things speak, and exhort, and rebuke with all authority. Let no man despise thee."

The closer we get to a light, the more defects we see because of that light. As we draw nigh to Christ, the Light of the world, we will see more defects in our hearts. God will continue to reveal the carbon dioxide. He will continue to reveal the things we need to push out from our lives by His grace. But while we are doing this, we also have to remember to breathe in. I believe the breath of revival is the breath of holiness. While we exhale sin, and that which is worldly, we need to inhale that which is holy.

God speaks about this often. Romans 12:1–2 says, "*I beseech you therefore, brethren, by the mercies of God, that ye present your bodies a living sacrifice, holy, acceptable unto God, which is your reasonable service. And be not conformed to this world: but be ye transformed by the renewing of your mind, that ye may prove what is that good, and acceptable, and perfect, will of God.*" In other words, we need to bring the new into our lives by first putting off the old.

First Peter 1:14–16 says, "*As obedient children, not fashioning yourselves according to the former lusts in your ignorance: But as he which hath called you is holy, so be ye holy in all manner of conversation; Because it is written, Be ye holy; for I am holy.*" God instructs us to keep ourselves pure. We must make sure we are breathing in good air. We must be breathing in the right kind of oxygen—the oxygen that is the holiness of God.

A student attending West Coast Baptist College recently handed me an article about happiness. This article focused on one major goal everyone has—to get the most happiness out of life. How wrong this goal is can be discovered instantly by meditatively reading through the New Testament once. One of the greatest dangers to holiness is the superficial myth of immediate happiness. In God's Word, the emphasis is not upon happiness, but upon holiness.

God is more concerned with the state of people's hearts than the state of people's feelings. Undoubtedly, the will of God brings final happiness to those who obey. But the most important matter is not how happy we are, but how holy we are. For those who would like to be serious about holiness, I have a suggestion. Go to God and tell Him that your desire is to be holy at any cost. Then ask Him to never give you more happiness than holiness, and when your holiness becomes tarnished, let your joy become dim. Ask Him to make you holy, whether or not you are happy, and be assured that in the end, you will be as happy as you are holy.

The Pattern of Holiness

There is a threefold prescription for holiness. Titus 2 shows us that holiness begins with a specific pattern. But before we study the pattern of holiness, we need to first meditate on wisdom from Paul in 2 Corinthians 10:12, *"For we dare not make ourselves of the number, or compare ourselves with some that commend themselves: but they measuring themselves by themselves, and comparing themselves among themselves, are not wise."*

It is very easy to compare ourselves with the average Christian, with those we work alongside, or with those with whom we associate. However, to compare ourselves or to measure ourselves with how the world is or how somebody else acts is not wise.

A Christian may look at the world and himself and see a major difference, but he fails to realize the world is moving. It is not static. The Bible says in 2 Timothy 3:13, *"But evil men and seducers shall wax worse and worse, deceiving, and being deceived."* This world is moving farther away from God. We are not evolving into something closer to God; we are devolving away from Him. Because the world is always moving, we would be foolish to compare ourselves to it. So the danger of comparing ourselves with one another, or comparing ourselves with the world and culture, is that it is not the supreme standard. The standard is shown through the pattern of holiness, outlined in the Word of God.

A Sound Pattern

Titus 2:1–2 says, *"But speak thou the things which become sound doctrine: That the aged men be sober, grave, temperate, sound in faith…."* Titus 2:8 mentions, *"Sound speech."* The Apostle Paul is describing a sound pattern; it is unmovable, remaining the same. This never-changing pattern is the Word of God.

Our world is changing, and our flesh hungers to change with it, but Isaiah 34:16 says, *"Seek ye out of the book of the Lord, and read: no one of these shall fail…."* God's Word is changeless. The psalmist says in Psalm 119:160, *"Thy word is true from the beginning: and every one of thy righteous judgments endureth for ever."* Psalm 119:89 says, *"For ever, O LORD, thy word is settled in heaven."* God's Word will still be the standard in Heaven. God's Word is eternal and forever; it does not change and cannot change. When earth is over and Heaven begins, it will still be the same. Isaiah 40:8 says, *"The grass withereth, the flower fadeth: but the word of our God shall stand for ever."* The pattern of holiness starts with a sound pattern.

A Spoken Pattern

Titus 2:1 and 3–4 continues to explain God's pattern of holiness: *"But speak thou the things which become sound doctrine. The aged women likewise, that they be in behaviour as becometh holiness, not false accusers, not given to much wine, teachers of good things; That they may teach...."* This pattern of holiness is not only sound, it is spoken. Titus 2:6 says, *"Young men likewise exhort"* Titus 2:9 continues, *"Exhort servants"* The terms, *"teach"* and *"exhort,"* mandate speech. Holiness must be taught, expounded, and exhorted.

When you feel apprehensive about attending a church in which the preacher exhorts you to live a separated life and maintain a relationship with God, your apprehension is a sign that you really don't want a Bible-based church. If you don't like it when a preacher stands at his pulpit and expounds on biblical principles of parenting, keeping standards, and having right relationships, then you really don't want a biblical ministry.

Basing every standard of living on the Bible is essential to live according to the will of God. If you shy away from this truth—neglecting the preachers who preach it, ignoring the Sunday school teachers who teach it, and neglecting the friends who live it—then you deliberately ignore part of God's plan for holiness. A spoken pattern is the speaking of holiness on a consistent basis.

"Cry aloud, spare not, lift up thy voice like a trumpet, and shew my people their transgression, and the house of Jacob their sins" (Isaiah 58:1). In Ezekiel 3:18, the Bible says, *"When I say unto the wicked, Thou shalt surely die, and thou givest him not warning, nor speakest to warn the wicked from his wicked way, to save his life; the same wicked man shall die in his iniquity; but his blood will I require at thine hand."* God commands the people of the church to speak the pattern.

A Shown Pattern

Someone once said, "Your walk talks and your talk talks but your walk talks louder than your talk talks." We could talk the talk all day long, but we need Christians to walk the walk. We need Christians who will live a pattern of holiness. Titus 2:7 says, *"In all things shewing thyself a pattern of good works: in doctrine shewing uncorruptness, gravity, sincerity."* Titus 2:10 continues to say, *"Not purloining, but shewing all good fidelity...."*

Parents can tell their children what to do, but they also need to show their children what to do. They need to show them the pattern by living the pattern. We can sit in church pews and hear the Bible preached, taught, and expounded upon; but, if we do not go out into the community and live the pattern of holiness, it is only shallow talk.

Paul said to Timothy in 1 Timothy 4:12, *"Let no man despise thy youth; but be thou an example of the believers, in word, in conversation, in charity, in spirit, in faith, in purity."* Simply put, Timothy was to be an example through his life.

My dad is now with the Lord. Through his life on this earth, he was never a man who talked much. They say the average male says 10,000 words a day. I don't think my dad said 10,000 words a week. Although he didn't talk much, he talked when he *needed* to talk. When he spoke, we listened because we knew what he had to say was important. My dad never said, "Son, let me teach you how to work." No, he showed me how to work. My parents never told us kids to get ready for church. We never asked if we were going to church; we only asked what time we were leaving for church. The pattern was always shown. We didn't ask if we were going to pray before our meals; we always prayed before a meal. That was the pattern of our family life.

What is your life's pattern like? Are you up and down, faithful to church one minute and missing the next? We must learn to have a consistent pattern of breathing properly—inhaling oxygen and exhaling carbon dioxide. We can experience revival meetings in a church and learn to breathe right, but how will our pattern be the week after the revival? We still need to get the carbon dioxide out and take in good and holy things. We must continue breathing properly, and if we do it long enough, we won't have to think about the process of inhaling and exhaling.

The Peculiarity of Holiness

Why does God demand that we be holy? Why is it so important to Him? If God is all-powerful and can do anything, why can't He just use us the way we are? We all have problems, deficiencies, and sinful baggage in our lives, but if God is all-powerful, shouldn't He be able to use us in spite of these problems? I encourage you to study the peculiarity of holiness.

A Debilitation of the Negative

Titus 2:8 gives us the first reason God requires holiness: "*Sound speech, that cannot be condemned; that he that is of the contrary part may be ashamed, having no evil thing to say of you."* God demands holiness from His people because He wants to debilitate the negative. He wants to purge the hypocrisy that exists.

Holiness eliminates hypocrisy. The world is watching us—those who are of the contrary part are watching us. Those who regularly breathe in the carbon dioxide are examining our every conversation and our every move. Oftentimes, the reason they don't want what we have is because of our inconsistency.

God demands a pattern of holiness because holiness is the key ingredient to becoming a peculiar Christian. During the week of a revival, your neighbors may see you leave your house, dressed up with a Bible in hand, and begin to wonder: *Oh, is it Wednesday? It is only Tuesday. Those folks have church on Wednesdays not on Tuesdays. Funny, I saw them go last night too. What's going on? These people are weird. Don't they have to be to work at 6:00 AM?*

You are debilitating the negative. The only way the world judges our Christianity is through what they see. God sees your heart, but the same verse which teaches that, also teaches that man looks on the outward appearance. First Samuel 16:7 says, *"…for man looketh on the outward appearance, but the LORD looketh on the heart."* God looks at the heart, and He sees our sincerity and our motives. He understands even if we mess up, but the problem is that our lives are the only "Bible" most people read. This is why Paul said in 2 Corinthians 3:2–3, *"Ye are our epistle written in our hearts, known and read of all men…written not with ink, but with the Spirit of the living God; not in tables of stone, but in fleshy tables of the heart."* Paul also says in 2 Corinthians 6:3, *"Giving no offence in any thing, that the ministry be not blamed."* When we don't live holy lives, the ministry gets blamed and God gets blamed. When Christianity gets blamed, those of a contrary part are repulsed.

It is one of God's most beautiful gifts to us when a soul reaches eternity because of our small influence. Imagine standing in Heaven and finding you were the reason some people were there. You may not always realize it, but every time you hand out a Gospel tract, every time you extend an invitation to your church, every time you preach Christ with your life, you are assisting God in the endeavor of sharing the truth with all people.

There may be a time when an altar worker gets to lead a visitor of yours to the Lord. You still had a part in his salvation. Those involved in the choir, the special music, the preaching, and the altar call all had a part in the salvation of his soul. I believe people will be surprised at the number of people in Heaven. What a glorious day it will be when we see the fruits of our labor. But the sobering day will be the day we realize there are people in Hell because of us.

It is common to have someone thank us for our help in leading them to Christ. They might say, "Hey, thanks for inviting me to church. I got saved today," or, "Thanks for teaching that lesson, it showed me that I do need Heaven." However, people who reject Christ rarely tell us of their decisions. All it takes is one little step off the beaten path, and they reject Christ because of our hypocrisy.

Your church is no stronger than its weakest member. Your pastor may be a wonderful preacher and your church may have powerful services that grip the heart, but the message is no stronger than what the world sees in your life. It is only a holy life that debilitates the negative. When your community sees people living holy lives, they will have no excuse to be unholy.

A Denial of the Natural

Titus 2:12 says, "*Teaching us that, denying ungodliness and worldly lusts….*" The holiness that comes into our lives denies the natural. Our flesh doesn't want to be holy. We may want to do right so we don't get into trouble, or we may strive to do good so we can be rewarded, but our flesh has no desire to do right. But a pattern of holiness denies the natural.

The Apostle Paul explains the battle that goes on in every one of us. Romans 7:14–17, 22–24 says, "*For we know that the law is spiritual: but I am carnal, sold under sin. For that which I do I allow not: for what I would, that do I not; but what I hate, that do I. If then I do that which I would not, I consent unto the law that it is good. Now then it is no more I that do it, but sin that dwelleth in me...For I delight in the law of God after the inward man: But I see another law in my members, warring against the law of my mind, and bringing me into captivity to the law of sin which is in my members. O wretched man that I am! Who shall deliver me from the body of this death?"*

Here was Paul, the great preacher, the great missionary, and the great statesman for God, who recognized the constant battle that rages within all of us—the battle between the flesh and the Spirit. In Galatians 5:16–17, the Bible says, "...*Walk in the Spirit, and ye shall not fulfill the lust of the flesh. For the flesh lusteth against the Spirit, and the Spirit against the flesh: and these are contrary the one to the other: so that ye cannot do the things that ye would.*" Naturally, our lives rebel against right. But when we develop a pattern of holiness in our lives, we will be able to deny the flesh.

An old Indian described this struggle in a powerful way. He said, "Inside of me there are two dogs fighting all the time. There's a white dog and there's a black dog that are always fighting. You may ask, which one wins? It's whatever one I feed the most."

Holiness feeds the Spirit. Jesus said in Matthew 16:24, "*If any man will come after me, let him deny himself, and take up his cross, and follow me."* If we live after the flesh, we shall die. But if we live after the Spirit, we shall live. Galatians 5:24 says, *"And they that are Christ's have crucified the flesh with the affections and lusts."* Paul said in Galatians 2:20, *"I am crucified with Christ: nevertheless I live; yet not I, but Christ liveth in me: and the life which I now live in the flesh I live by the faith of the Son of God, who loved me, and gave himself for me."* Paul died daily. He committed spiritual suicide daily. Everyday, you and I need to get into the pattern of holiness by putting our flesh on the altar of death. We need to put our agendas and our desires to death. To be crucified with Christ is a denial of the natural.

The Discovery of the Needful

It is needful for us to live righteously in this world! Titus 2:12 says, *"Teaching us that, denying ungodliness and worldly lusts, we should live soberly, righteously, and godly, in this present world."* God puts this together in a composite sentence: *"Awake to righteousness and sin not"* (1 Corinthians 15:34). This is spiritual breathing. Exhale and get the carbon dioxide out, but inhale righteousness and sin not.

Psalm 1:1–2 says, *"Blessed is the man that walketh not in the counsel of the ungodly, nor standeth in the way of sinners, nor sitteth in the seat of the scornful. But his delight is in the law of the LORD; and in his law doth he meditate day and night.*" Ephesians 4:22–24 says, "*That ye put off concerning the former conversation the old man, which is corrupt according to the deceitful lusts; And be renewed in the spirit of your mind; And that ye put on the new man, which after God is created in righteousness and true holiness.*" Putting off and putting on—this is the process of spiritual breathing. "*Therefore if any man be in Christ, he is a new creature: old things are passed away; behold, all things are become new*" (2 Corinthians 5:17).

Putting off is easy to talk about, but difficult to actually do. If you visited my office and turned on my computer, the first thing that would pop up is a picture of my grandkids. Then you would see folders popping up on my desktop. I know this could cause a computer crash, but there are about fifty folders on my desktop.

Why do I need these folders on my desktop? Because they remind me of things I have to do every day. The things that are on my desktop are important. I won't be able to find what I need to get done every day if I have to search for those folders. I need them to be staring at me every day. I want those things right where I can see them. I want to be reminded of those things that are important in my life.

Up on the left side of my screen is a trash can. If I wanted to find information I had sent to the trash, I would have to click the icon and pull the information back out, but I don't make a habit of going through the garbage. The information is there; it is still in my computer, but it is put away in the trash.

Our brains work the same way. We can put filth in, and be forgiven, and washed before God, but the truth is, humanly, until we get new bodies and new minds, it is still there. This is a fact of life. I wish it were different. I wish that when we confess our sin, we could forget our sin. God does, but we can't. It's there, and since the devil knows it's there, he will keep bringing it back to our attention.

Do you wonder why you struggle so much with a certain sin? Have you considered that maybe you have not put that sin in the trash? It may be that every time your brain comes on, you see the wrong. In order to make things right, you must repent. You must take what is wrong and drag it over to the trash and then you must start putting information on the desktop that will remind you of holiness. When you decide to put off, you need to make a simultaneous decision to put on.

If all you do is throw sin in the trash, guess what? The devil will have more trash for you to be tempted with next week. If you just breathe out carbon dioxide, you'll soon faint and die. You need to breathe normally. You need to drag the old out and establish a pattern of holiness.

The Preparation for Holiness

Holiness Prepares Us for the Happy Appearing of Christ

Holiness has enormous ramifications for the present, but it also prepares us for the future. Holiness prepares us for the happy appearing of Christ. Titus 2:13 says, *"Looking for that blessed hope, and the glorious appearing of the great God and our Saviour Jesus Christ."* Christ is coming back for us. First Thessalonians 4:13–18 teaches, *"But I would not have you to be ignorant, brethren, concerning them which are asleep, that ye sorrow not, even as others which have no hope. For if we believe that Jesus died and rose again, even so them also which sleep in Jesus will God bring with him. For this we say unto you by the word of the Lord, that we which are alive and remain unto the coming of the Lord shall not prevent them which are asleep. For the Lord himself shall descend from heaven with a shout, with the voice of the archangel, and with the trump of God: and the dead in Christ shall rise first: Then we which are alive and remain shall be caught up together with them in the clouds, to meet the Lord in the air: and so shall we ever be with the Lord. Wherefore comfort one another with these words."*

The coming of Christ ought to bring comfort to our hearts. But if we are not living holy lives, His appearing will not be comforting. Suppose you leave church with your family, and you realize that because of such a busy day, you forgot to eat. You decide to take the kids home before you and your wife get something quick to eat. After telling your children not to watch TV or talk on the phone, but go straight to bed, you and your wife drive to your favorite fast food place.

After ordering at the counter, you realize you forgot your wallet. So, you both get back in the car and travel home to get your wallet. It has only been five minutes since you left, and you and your wife walk into the house only to find some of your kids watching TV, and one with a phone dangling from her ear. Now will your arrival home earlier than expected be a comfort to your children? Not if you are the right kind of parent! They were doing what you clearly said *not* to do, and they were *not* doing what you said *to* do.

Jesus told us He is coming back, and we are to comfort one another with these words. Are we living in such a way that it would be a comfort for Christ to return? First John 2:28 says, "*And now, little children, abide in him; that, when he shall appear, we may have confidence, and not be ashamed before him at his coming.*" Living a holy life prepares us for the happy appearing of Christ.

Holiness Prepares Us for the Honorable Approval of Christ

Holiness prepares us for an honorable approval of Christ. Titus 2:14 says, "*Who gave himself for us, that he might* redeem us from all iniquity, and purify unto himself a peculiar people, zealous of good works." We are bought with a price. Paul said in 2 Corinthians 11:2, "*For I am jealous over you with godly jealousy: for I have espoused you to one husband, that I may present you as a chaste virgin to Christ.*" Paul's desire was to present his fellow Christians blameless, chaste, and pure before God. He wanted them to be approved of Christ.

Every man's work will soon be made manifest. Are you living a life that is worthy of the honorable approval of Christ? Holiness is the one essence that will prepare us for what Ecclesiastes 12:14 prophecies, "*For God shall bring every work into judgment, with every secret thing; whether it be good, or whether it be evil.*" It is a holy life that prepares us for an honorable approval.

Holiness Prepares Us for a Heavenly Association with Christ

One humbling thought is found in Titus 2:14, "*…that he might redeem us from all iniquity, and purify unto himself….*" Isn't it amazing that God wants to associate with us, and He wants to associate with us forever?

Did you know Jesus prayed for us in John 17:15–21? He prayed for those who would be saved. "*I pray not that thou shouldest take them out of the world, but that thou shouldest keep them from the evil. They are not of the world, even as I am not of the world, Sanctify them through thy truth: thy word is truth. As thou hast sent me into the world, even so have I also sent them into the world. And for their sakes I sanctify myself, that they also might be sanctified through the truth. Neither pray I for these alone, but for them also which shall believe on me through their word; That they all may be one; as thou, Father, art in me, and I in thee, that they also may be one in us: that the world may believe that thou hast sent me."* Jesus prayed that God would keep us from evil because we are one with the Lord. Holiness prepares us for a heavenly association with Christ.

First John 3:1–3 promises, *"Behold, what manner of love the Father hath bestowed upon us, that we should be called the sons of God: therefore the world knoweth us not, because it knew him not. Beloved, now are we the sons of God, and it doth not yet appear what we shall be: but we know that, when he shall appear, we shall be like him; for we shall see him as he is. And every man that hath this hope in him purifieth himself, even as he is pure."* We are going to be His forever!

Salvation is the starting point. It doesn't matter where you start, just as long as you do. Some may have been saved at four years old, and others may be reading their Bibles for the first time at fifty. The starting point can begin anywhere, because God will find and save you at any age no matter where you are in life.

Glorification is the finishing point. When we get to Heaven we will be glorified. We will be like Christ. It is humbling to realize that one day, we will be like our Creator.

Sanctification is the growing point. When we first enter God's family, we are still somewhat close to the starting point—we still have areas in our lives where God needs to work. Old things are passing away, and all things are becoming new. We are becoming new creatures in Christ. At salvation, we may not have realized all that God had planned for our lives after salvation. Sanctification is growing—walking with the Lord. Sanctification is putting off the carbon dioxide and turning our backs on our old ways. Soon, we begin to detest the carbon dioxide more and more, putting distance between the world and us. Our desire to become more like Christ grows. If you are saved, you are at this growing point of sanctification.

If Jesus came today, how much distance would there still be to glorification? What would God have wanted to change that you didn't allow Him to change? Wouldn't you like to be as close to the glorification point as possible?

There is a gap between where you are and where glorification stands. What is in your gap? This is what the judgment is all about—it's about the gap.

Do you want to know what revival is? Revival is narrowing this gap. For some, it might be one big step, and for others, it might be several small steps. It's the normal process of breathing right—getting rid of the old and putting on the new.

Paul Haley was a little boy living in Denver, Colorado battling an incurable disease. He was dying, and the doctors gave him no hope. Various foundations, including the Make-a-Wish Foundation, visited him at home. It was learned that Paul Haley's desire as a little boy was to meet President Eisenhower, a former General and President of the United States at that time.

A reporter in Denver, Colorado, heard about the story and sent a letter to President Eisenhower, knowing that he was going to be visiting Denver. The President was touched and moved by the story. After his meeting, unannounced, he said to his security detail, "Before we go to the airport, I have an address I want to go to." Security changed their plans and loaded the cars with the President and his bodyguards and made their way to a subdivision in Denver.

They found the address and pulled their motorcade to a stop. President Dwight Eisenhower strode up the sidewalk to a medium-sized home in a subdivision and knocked on the door.

Donald Haley, Paul's father had slept in that Saturday morning. He was tired after a long week of work. When he got up, he didn't bother to shave or brush his teeth. He just threw on a pair of sweats and a T-shirt and decided to relax. His hair was disheveled;

the growth of his beard was obvious. When he heard the knock on the door, he opened the door, and there stood the President of the United States. The media began to take pictures as little Paul Haley was brought out to meet the President. Later Donald Haley was interviewed and through his tears, he said, "If only I had been prepared. I'm so ashamed that I opened that door in a pair of sweatpants and a T-shirt. If I had only known he was coming, I would have been prepared."

The Bible tells us in Amos 4:12 to, "...*prepare to meet thy God.*" He is coming again, and the closer we are to Him at that point in time, the greater that reunion will be with Him.

CHAPTER FIVE

The Blessings of Revival

Have you ever been ripped off? Have you ever bought something and later thought, "*What was I thinking?*" About twenty years ago, we had just had our third child, and we were traveling as a family in a single cab pickup truck with a trailer. It was a good truck. It had a good engine and was in good condition, but it had limited seating. My wife, our three kids, our dog, and myself were all supposed to fit on one long seat. Because it was getting crowded, I began to look for a quad cab truck.

Today, they are called quad trucks, but in those days they were called gas shortages. Nobody was selling this kind of truck. They had huge engines. Chevy had 454s, and Ford had 460s. Basically, they had stopped making them. You couldn't find them anywhere.

I looked every place I'd go. I looked in newspapers, at car lots, out soulwinning. For months I searched, and then one day, something caught my eye while I was out visiting with a good pastor friend of mine. We were traveling by a dealership in Lapeer, Michigan, and I saw it. It was shiny and beautiful. I asked the pastor if we could pull into the dealership and look at a truck.

We pulled into the dealership, and of course, the salesman came running to greet us. We began examining the truck. It was older, but the mileage was only at 66,000. The price for this 454 engine was even lower than I expected. I called my bank back home and made arrangements. I had found the truck for which I had been searching! The salesman worked with me, and I was able to trade in my truck, as well as get a loan from the bank. I was thrilled! Finally, I felt like a real evangelist. My whole family could fit comfortably in our new truck as we traveled from church to church.

The following week was busy, and I was trying to get all of the wiring hooked up from the trailer to our new truck before the weekend came. Friday night I was anxious to finally hook the trailer up and head down the highway. I was so excited that we now had a truck that could meet our family's needs. My family and I started to the next meeting, which was about 500 miles away in Tomah, Wisconsin.

By the time we arrived, we had no brakes. We were relying on the trailer brakes to stop. We pulled into the church in Wisconsin, and when the pastor met us, he began to admire my truck. As he was admiring, I was doubting.

Early that week, I took my truck in to get its brakes fixed. Not only were the brakes shot, the drums had been turned, and both sides had been used. After telling the mechanic there were only 66,000 miles on the truck, he looked at me amused and told me that was impossible. He estimated that the truck either had 166,000 or maybe even 266,000 miles on it, and it had also been repainted!

The brake job cost me $1,000. The following week, I paid $1,500 for a new transmission. This spending expenditure continued for four weeks. The cheapest bill I received for that truck was $600. I began to call that truck the Pharisee. It looked good on the outside, but that was it! I would go out in the morning and say, "How are ya doing, Pharisee?" I would look at that truck, and think about how much I got ripped off. That salesman in Lapeer is probably still laughing today.

The devil is also a cunning salesman. Hebrews 11:25 says there are, "...*pleasures of sin for a season.*" Proverbs 15:21 says, "*Folly is joy to him that is destitute of wisdom:*" Don't give the devil opportunity to laugh at you for taking pleasure in his sin for a season. Sin is a rip off.

Unlike sin, revival is not a rip off. If we will do what God wants us to do; if we desire to be spiritual, breathing New Testament Christians, there will be a cost. Revival costs something. It is not for the casual Christian, for it has a price. Revival is not easy. It is never easy to give up something or surrender something when the Holy Spirit convicts the heart. The Bible has a cost—it doesn't come cheap and the cost isn't free.

With that known, is it worth it? Is revival worth the cost? Is it worth the price we must pay to continue revival? God may be making some strong demands in your life. He may be asking you to confess some tough sins. He may be asking you to restore some relationships that are very difficult to confront. Second Corinthians 5 shows us five wonderful blessings that God gives us through revival. It is worth it!

A Demolished Past

A Constraining Love

Our past is demolished because of a constraining love. Isn't it amazing that God loves us? The psalmist says, *"When I consider thy heavens, the work of thy fingers, the moon and the stars, which thou hast ordained; What is man, that thou art mindful of him? and the son of man, that thou visitest him?"* (Psalm 8:3–4).

There is nothing in us humanly that is attractive to God. Nothing. The Apostle Paul said in Romans 7:18, *"For I know that in me (that is, in my flesh,) dwelleth no good thing...."* When God sees the human race, He sees none righteous. Romans 3:10–12 says, *"...There is none righteous, no, not one: There is none that understandeth, there is none that seeketh after God. They are all gone out of the way, they are together become unprofitable; there is none that doeth good, no, not one."* Yet the Bible says in Lamentations 3:22–23, *"It is of the LORD's mercies that we are not consumed, because his compassions fail not. They are new every morning: great is thy faithfulness."* Although we are nothing but filthy rags, it is God's compelling love for us that demolishes our past.

A Changed Life

When God saved us, He didn't just reform the old; He regenerated our lives. Second Corinthians 5:17 says, *"Therefore if any man be in Christ, he is a new creature: old things are passed away; behold, all things are become new."* God is not interested in reformation. He is not interested in helping us turn over a new leaf. The Bible says in Ezekiel 36:26, *"A new heart also will I give you, and a new spirit will I put within you...."* When God saved us, He gave us brand new hearts and a brand new Spirit. God doesn't just try to "fix up" our ways. God starts over, and that is why He calls it being "born again." Colossians 3:10 says, *"And have put on the new man, which is renewed in knowledge after the image of him that created him."*

Whenever I think of God's power to change a life completely, I think of a man named Mel Trotter. Mel was addicted to alcohol. He was a drunk who spent most of his time in a saloon. His wife began to expect his outrages, his violent tantrums, and even his threats.

One particular evening, Mel staggered home late into the night. His wife met him at the door with big tears in her eyes. She began to plead with her drunken husband for their baby's life. The baby was sick and had been running a dangerous fever. Without medicine, their baby didn't have a chance. Mel's wife begged him to go to the drugstore and buy medicine.

Mel Trotter didn't have any money; he bought a drink with every dime he ever put in his pocket. Cautiously, his wife opened the kitchen cabinet and pulled open a small drawer. Inside the drawer, she picked up a little jar she had stashed away without her husband's knowing. There were only a few bills and coins saved, but it would be enough to buy the medicine. She pulled out the money and placed it into her husband's hands. She pleaded and begged him to go straight to the store and come right home. Mel sobered at the words of his wife and headed out the door, money in hand.

He began walking to the drugstore with every intention of helping his little girl. But as he was walking, he passed by a saloon and his thirst for liquor was so great that he veered inside and spent the money on more booze. Staggering through the door of their apartment hours later, his wife met him with news that their baby girl was dead.

At the funeral, before the casket was closed, Mel reached down and untied his baby girl's shoes. He pulled them off of her feet and put them in his pocket. An hour after the casket had been safely lowered into the grave; Mel Trotter went to the nearest pawnshop and exchanged her shoes for more liquor.

Sin took its toll, and Mel sank deeper and deeper into sin's stronghold. One night Mel was walking the streets of Chicago, headed toward a bridge near Lake Michigan, where he planned to commit suicide. His life was worthless, over, and ruined by drink. He decided to end it all. As he was walking toward the bridge, he heard music and singing. He looked and saw lights, and a sign that read, "Pacific Garden Mission."

By the miraculous grace of God, Mel Trotter went inside and sat in the back row.

He heard a preacher preach on the love of God, and during the invitation call, Mel Trotter left his seat, walked down the aisle, and trusted Jesus Christ as his Saviour. God not only saved Mel Trotter that night, but He also quenched his thirst for booze. Mel Trotter went back to his hometown in Grand Rapids, Michigan. It was there that he opened a rescue mission to reach people just like him. In his lifetime, Mel Trotter started sixty-six rescue missions all across this nation. Why? Because, God changed his life.

Mel's life was never the same; God demolished his past by changing his life and making him a new man in Christ. This is a small slice of the whole blessing God gives in revival. Mel could finally say, "The things I used to do, I don't do them anymore," because of a constraining love and a changed life.

A Diminishing Present

Revival takes the luster off of this world. Things that were so important to us before, begin to fade. Things that took priority in our lives before, don't look interesting anymore. When revival hits, our priorities change!

An Emptiness of the Earthly

When revival comes into our lives, the things that were so important when we were away from God suddenly become tarnished. They don't attract us anymore. Even Solomon said in Proverbs 14:13, "*Even in laughter the heart is sorrowful, and the end of that mirth is heaviness.*" Proverbs 16:25 says, "*There is a way that seemeth right unto a man….*" When we are away from God, that way looks so right to us; but when there is a revival, this world and all it has to offer looks empty.

Again, Solomon, who had everything his eyes desired, said in Ecclesiastes 2:11, "*Then I looked on all the works that my hands had wrought, and on the labour that I had laboured to do; and, behold, all was vanity and vexation of spirit, and there was no profit under the sun.*" Second Corinthians 5:1 says, "*For we know that if our earthly house of this tabernacle were dissolved, we have a building of God, an house not made with hands, eternal in the heavens.*"

An Envy of the Eternal

Revival ignites a longing inside of us to be with God. When we experience revival, we will long to leave this life and live with Him eternally. Second Corinthians 5:2 says, "*For in this we groan, earnestly desiring to be clothed upon with our house which is from heaven.*" The psalmist said in Psalm 73:25, "*Whom have I in heaven but thee? and there is none upon earth that I desire beside thee.*" Psalm 42:2 says, "*My soul thirsteth for God, for the living God: when shall I come and appear before God?*" Psalm 63:1 says, "*O God, thou art my God; early will I seek thee: my soul thirsteth for thee, my flesh longeth for thee in a dry and thirsty land, where no water is.*"

When our souls are revived, we are no longer thirsty for the world or sin. We are no longer hungry for the things of the flesh. We have a new thirst—a thirst for God. Church services are important once again, and the meat of God's Word is more important to us than any physical food we could possibly intake. As Job said in Job 23:12, "*I have esteemed the words of his mouth more than my necessary food.*" Jeremiah 15:16 says, "*Thy words were found, and I did eat them; and thy word was unto me the joy and rejoicing of mine heart: for I am called by thy name, O LORD God of hosts.*" Revival will exhort our souls to envy God's eternal Word and our eternal home in Heaven.

An Evidence of the Enemy

Second Corinthians 5:4 continues to explain the diminishing present: "*For we that are in this tabernacle do groan, being burdened: not for that we would be unclothed, but clothed upon, that mortality might be swallowed up of life.*" When revival comes, we become burdened by this old tabernacle. We are burdened by this old flesh. We suddenly realize that this old flesh is not what we want. Before revival, we love the flesh; but when revival comes, we loathe the flesh. "*O wretched man that I am!*" Paul said in Romans 7:24, "*who shall deliver me from the body of this death?*" Paul recognized the enemy—because his heart was revived, his heart was right.

Isaiah, when he saw the Lord high and lifted up, said in Isaiah 6:5, "*...Woe is me! for I am undone; because I* *am a man of unclean lips, and I dwell in the midst of a people of unclean lips: for mine eyes have seen the King, the* LORD *of hosts.*"

An Excitement for an Exit

Second Corinthians 5:6 says, "*Therefore we are always confident, knowing that, whilst we are at home in the body, we are absent from the Lord.*" While we are in this body, we are absent from God. We want the eternal, but we are stuck here in the earthly. Second Corinthians 5:7–8 says, "*(For we walk by faith, not by sight:) We are confident, I say, and willing rather to be absent from the body, and to be present with the Lord.*"

With revival comes a desire to be with the Lord. There will be a desire to be absent from the flesh and have a glorified body with Him. Paul said in 1 Corinthians 15:51–57, "*Behold, I shew you a mystery; We shall not all sleep, but we shall all be changed, In a moment, in the twinkling of an eye, at the last trump: for the trumpet shall sound, and the dead shall be raised incorruptible, and we shall be changed. For this corruptible must put on incorruption, and this mortal must put on immortality. So when this corruptible shall have put on incorruption, and this mortal shall have put on immortality, then shall be brought to pass the saying that is written, Death is swallowed up in victory. O death, where is thy sting? O grave, where is thy victory? The sting of death is sin; and the strength of sin is the law. But thanks be to God, which giveth us the victory through our Lord Jesus Christ."*

We will look forward to the change that takes place when Jesus comes—when we are absent from the body and present with the Lord. Philippians 3:20–21 says, *"For our conversation is in heaven; from whence also we look for the Saviour, the Lord Jesus Christ: Who shall change our vile body, that it may be fashioned like unto his glorious body, according to the working whereby he is able even to subdue all things unto himself."* This is why Paul said in Philippians 1:21, *"For to me to live is Christ, and to die is gain."*

If God leaves me here clothed in the flesh, clothed in the old body, clothed in the old tabernacle, I'm going to live for Him. But I can't wait until I die, because that day will be a promotion. Paul couldn't wait for his exit from this earth and his promotion to Heaven. He couldn't wait for the call. He couldn't wait for the trumpet to sound! Even so, we should have an excitement about our exit to a better place.

A Divine Presence

A Holy Ambition

Second Corinthians 5:9 says, *"Wherefore we labour, that, whether present or absent, we may be accepted of him."* Revival brings us closer to the one who is holy.

It takes the focus off of pleasing self and places it on pleasing God.

Jesus said in John 8:29, "*...I do always those things that please him.*" I would like to finish a day just once and be able to say I did everything in that day to please Him. It hasn't happened yet, but it ought to be everyone's goal. When revival comes, that is the desire. It is no longer about pleasing me, pleasing others, or being accepted by the crowd. It is about being accepted by God—we have a holy ambition. Philippians 3:10, "*That I may know him, and the power of his resurrection, and the fellowship of his sufferings, being made conformable unto his death.*" Paul said in 1 Thessalonians 4:1, "*...as ye have received of us how ye ought to walk and to please God, so ye would abound more and more.*" God's divine presence in revival gives us an ambition to be holy. Whether we are present or absent, whether we are alive or dead, whether we are with the Lord or here on this earth, it doesn't matter. Our desire should be to be accepted of Him.

An Honest Accountability

Someone asked Daniel Webster what the greatest thought is that can occupy one's mind. Daniel Webster replied that the greatest thought that can occupy a man's mind is his accountability to God. What keeps us in God's divine presence is understanding that while revival meetings come and go, we are daily walking with God, and we will give an honest accounting to Him one day.

Second Corinthians 5:10 says, "*For we must all appear before the judgment seat of Christ; that every one may receive the things done in his body, according to that he hath done, whether it be good or bad.*" One day, what is perceived about your life will no longer matter. Perception will no longer be reality. Reality will be reality. When you stand before the Lord, you won't be judged by your reputation. You will be judged honestly by who you *really* are.

If any thought could keep us accountable and motivate us to be right with God, it is knowing that one day we will give an honest account to God.

A Devoted Purpose

When revival comes, our aim, our mission, our purpose for life is different. Colossians 3:1–2 says, "*If ye then be risen with Christ, seek those things which are above, where Christ sitteth on the right hand of God. Set your affection on things above, not on things on the earth.*" Matthew 6:33 tells us to "*…seek ye first the kingdom of God, and his righteousness; and all these things shall be added unto you.*" Before revival, we are concerned about earthly things—jobs, money, retirement, savings accounts, and electric bills! These earthly burdens consume our lives. But when revival comes, we have a different purpose. God is no longer prominent, He becomes preeminent! He's not just in first place; He is in all the places.

A Ministry of Persuasion

Second Corinthians 5:11 says, "*Knowing therefore the terror of the Lord, we persuade men….*" When God revives us, we will have the desire to tell others of Christ and share the message of how He changed our lives. Before revival, we don't care. When we run into people at the gas station or in the store, we don't care whether or not they are saved. All we care about is that we, along with our families, are going to Heaven. But when revival floods into our lives, we have a new ministry of persuasion.

Have you ever persuaded others to come to church by saying, "You wouldn't want to come to our church, would you? Our pastor is loud and sometimes he preaches long, too." Is that how you would persuade someone? Now I am not saying that you should cram something down somebody's throat or buttonhole them. The truth is *you* are not the soulwinner. *God* is the soulwinner, but we are the messengers. However, if the messenger is not convinced about his message, why would he expect anyone to want what he has? If someone had a message to share with me that required

action on my part, I would want to be convinced that
he believes in what he is saying. I would want him to
show me that he means what he is saying. Paul said in
Romans 9:1–3, "*I say the truth in Christ, I lie not, my
conscience also bearing me witness in the Holy Ghost,
That I have great heaviness and continual sorrow in
my heart. For I could wish that myself were accursed
from Christ for my brethren, my kinsmen according to
the flesh.*" Do you know what Paul was saying? Paul's
burden for his people was so great, he wished that he
could trade places with his nation so that they would be
saved, and he would go to Hell. Paul was serious about
persuading others with the message of Christ—he was
willing to sacrifice his eternity for their salvation. Paul
demonstrated a ministry of persuasion.

When something changes our lives, we don't have
a problem promoting it to others. When Christ does a
work in our lives—when He revives us—we will want
to go out as often as possible and persuade others. We
will make it a priority to win souls. We will do what
it takes to rearrange our schedules to make time for
telling others of Christ, and we will have a ministry of
persuasion.

A Ministry of Performance

We should purpose to not only tell others about
Christ, but also to daily perform God's will for our

lives. Second Corinthians 5:15 says, *"And that he died for all, that they which live should not henceforth live unto themselves, but unto him which died for them; and rose again."* Our desire and our purpose should be to *live* for God; therefore, it is not enough to simply know what is right—we must perform that which is right as well.

Paul said in 2 Corinthians 8:11, *"Now therefore perform the doing of it; that as there was a readiness to will, so there may be a performance also out of that which ye have."* As God shows you the truth of His Word and His will, you must start living it out. When God gives us something, we are required to be good stewards of it. First Corinthians 4:2 says, *"It is required in stewards that a man be found faithful."* In the midst of God's goodness and favor upon our lives, we ought to be found faithful stewards of all that He gives us. We should strive to be *"...stedfast, unmoveable, always abounding in the work of the Lord"* (1 Corinthians 15:58).

One man had a major influence on my life as a teenager. He was very patient with me. He was a pastor who held youth rallies and directed a camp which my church often attended. Although this man had a great influence on my life, as a teenager, I didn't want to admit it. I thought he was too old-fashioned, old, and to be honest, I thought he was weird.

He is now in his eighties and is still pastoring the same church. Only one word is needed to describe him—faithful. He is a faithful man of God. I spent time with him recently, and I was commending him for a moment about his faithfulness, when he looked at me with tears in his eyes and said, "You know, Brother Goetsch, I just tried to be faithful. I never had a big church; I've pastored in a small Wisconsin town that's bent on pleasure and booze. It's not been easy, but I've tried to be faithful. As far as I know, I've never in my sixty years of ministry, missed a week of door knocking. Even when I go on vacation, I try to knock on a few doors."

If I introduced you to this man, you would not be impressed. If you visited his church, you would probably be disappointed with the building or the size of the crowd. But the older I get, the more I admire faithfulness. A long time ago, revival took place in that pastor's heart which has lasted for sixty years of his life.

A Ministry of Prayer

The third purpose that comes into our lives as a result of revival is selfless prayer. Second Corinthians 5:20 says, "*Now then we are ambassadors for Christ, as though God did beseech you by us: we pray you in Christ's stead, be ye reconciled to God.*" Before revival, our prayers are often focused on ourselves. We may not pray in a selfish way, but we simply know we need it. Praying this way is not wrong. But this type of prayer—humbling ourselves before Him and pleading for His working in our lives—is what moves God to work in our hearts.

When revival takes place, prayer becomes a product of that revival—our prayers begin to focus on others. We begin to claim a neighborhood in our prayers; we claim a city, an offering to give, or a building to build. We begin to pray that God will use us to influence others for His glory. We begin to focus in on our prayers; they are more specific, and we have a devoted purpose in our prayer life.

A Dependent Power

Second Corinthians 5:21 says, "*For he hath made him to be sin for us, who knew no sin; that we might be made the righteousness of God in him.*" Where do we get the power to continue revival? Where do we get the strength to continue what God has done? Second Corinthians 3:5 says, "*Not that we are sufficient of ourselves to think any thing as of ourselves; but our sufficiency is of God.*" Jesus reminds us in John 15:5, "*…for without me ye can do nothing.*"

When we begin to start breathing in a holy life and exhaling sin, our spiritual strength begins to be restored. Revival restores our respiration, and power begins to return to our spiritual bodies. The power to continue revival in our lives comes from one source alone.

God's Power in Salvation

How did you get saved? You couldn't save yourself through works or any other means; you had to depend upon God's power for salvation. Titus 3:5 says, *"Not by works of righteousness which we have done, but according to his mercy he saved us, by the washing of regeneration, and renewing of the Holy Ghost."* Romans 11:6 says, *"… if by grace, then is it no more of works: otherwise grace is no more grace. But if it be of works, then is it no more grace: otherwise work is no more work."*

We have no power to save ourselves; we only have the ability to accept God's saving power for our lives. We cannot neglect the fact that we are sinners, nor can we get to Heaven on our own. Ephesians 2:8–9 says, *"For by grace are ye saved through faith; and that not of yourselves: it is the gift of God: Not of works, lest any man should boast."* We are saved through faith in Christ. First Peter 1:18–19 says, *"Forasmuch as ye know that ye were not redeemed with corruptible things, as silver and gold, from your vain conversation received by tradition from your fathers; But with the precious blood of Christ, as of a lamb without blemish and without spot."*

Jesus said, *"…I am the way, the truth, and the life: no man cometh unto the Father, but by me"* (John 14:6). Acts 4:12 says, *"Neither is there salvation in any other: for there is none other name under heaven given among men, whereby we must be saved."* Isaiah 43:11 says, *"I,*

even I, am the LORD; and beside me there is no saviour."
The power of salvation comes from God alone.

God's Power in Service

How will we have the strength to serve in the ministry?
Where will we get this power to serve? God's power
not only gives us salvation, it also enables us to serve.
Neither you nor I can keep a revival going. Only God's
power can bring and sustain revival.

Philippians 4:13 says, *"I can do all things through
Christ which strengtheneth me."* How are we going to
experience revival daily in our lives? Through Christ.
How are we going to have boldness to go soulwinning?
Through Christ. How are we going to make it financially
and still give to the local church? Through Christ. How
are we going to accomplish something for God in our
families? Through Christ. Just as we depend on God's
power for salvation, we must depend on His power to
serve Him.

Remember the story I shared of getting ripped off
when I purchased a truck to accommodate my family?
You would agree with me that I made a mistake. It was
a big mistake, and I ended up paying for it in the end.
Although revival comes with a cost, when you add the
blessings of God, it is completely worth it.

Years ago, I was preaching one morning at a summer
camp in Wyoming on the subject of dating. This always

seems to be a safe topic with teenagers. They always have a need for it, and they seem to have an appetite to listen better when I preach on this subject.

That evening, I came down for supper in the dining hall. A young lady counselor was waiting, and it was obvious she had been crying. Her eyes were weary and red. She was still wiping her tears when she looked at me and said, "May I talk with you?"

"Sure." I replied. We walked over to one side of the eating area. She held out her hand to me, and inside her hand was a diamond ring.

"Brother Goetsch, do you see this?"

"Yes, it is a beautiful diamond ring. It looks expensive," I said.

"It was about five thousand dollars," she said, as her head began to lower.

"Why is it in your hand and not on your finger?" I asked.

"Brother Goetsch, I am in Bible college. My fiancé and I have told each other we love each other. We are engaged to be married, but it's just not right. It hasn't been a spiritual relationship. Oh, we haven't been immoral or anything. It's just too much emphasis on the physical rather than the spiritual. This morning, God spoke to my heart, and I know what we have to do. Since I was a little girl, I dreamed of getting married. I have had my wedding planned since I was five years old, and I look forward to that day. But it's not right. The camp director has given me permission to fly home tonight and give this ring back. Brother Goetsch, I don't think there is anything I have done that is harder than this. Will you please pray for me?"

We prayed together. I left camp later that week not knowing how the situation came to be. Months passed, years passed, even a whole decade passed. I was preaching in Laurel, Montana. It was the first night of a revival, and I was greeting the church folks. As I was standing in the back shaking hands, out of the corner of my eye, I saw a family. There was a very tall man, about six feet nine inches tall. He was wearing boots, jeans, a big belt buckle, a cowboy shirt, and had a cowboy hat in his hand. A lady was standing next to him along with three boys at her side.

Feeling a little apprehensive with these people standing there, I continued to shake as many hands as I could. Soon there was nobody else except that family in the church. I turned around, and they walked toward me. I tried to make small talk and asked them how they were doing.

"You don't remember me, do you?" the lady asked.

"No ma'am, I don't think so."

She smiled and said, "Pinedale, Wyoming. Red Cliff Bible Camp."

My memory was sparked, and I remembered that young counselor I had talked to years before. I was glad to see her and asked how she had been.

"Remember," she said, "How I said that breaking up with my fiancé was the hardest thing I'd ever do? Look what I got in its place," she said as she introduced me to her kind husband and her three boys.

At the end of that night, I could see how God allowed her to sacrifice something that was good for something that was best. There were great rewards waiting for this young lady, and she received those rewards by obediently following the Master's leading.

Not too long ago, I was preaching in a town in Indiana. I was sitting on the platform when the pastor asked if anyone in the congregation had a testimony. One man named Jim raised his hand. He stood up and began to share his heart. He told the congregation that twenty years prior he had heard a man preach at a camp on the topic of dating. He was only in seventh grade and did not like what the preacher was saying. He thought the preacher was crazy for preaching on principles that nobody followed anymore. Everybody in the church knew of the story that Jim told—He had married an unsaved girl, divorced, and his life became one wreck after another. This man ended his testimony by wishing he had listened to that message over twenty years ago, and acknowledging that, he didn't, he paid an awful price.

Jim is not in church; he is living for the world. Allow me to ask you, twenty years from this moment, will you regret not giving your heart to God? After reading through this book, will you look back and think, I wish I had listened?

How much is revival worth to you? Would you rather have the shiny ring, or would you give that immediate pleasure to God and wait for His blessings instead? God is not trying to rip you off. He wants to pour out His blessings of revival on you. Don't hold on to your diamond ring when God's blessings of revival are in your reach.

Conclusion

Revival cannot be manufactured or produced by man-made methodology and manipulation. It is heaven-sent. John 3:27 says, *"A man can receive nothing, except it be given him from heaven."* Without God we are nothing and can do nothing, for we are not *"sufficient of ourselves to think any thing as of ourselves; but our sufficiency is of God"* (2 Corinthians 3:5).

The Bible is filled with the testimonies of men and women who were used of God to do His work. They were no different than you and I, yet as they yielded themselves to the control of an all-powerful God, they made a difference in their generations. And in every generation since, God has raised up countless others to take the baton of truth and pass it on to those around them.

Now it's our turn! This is our generation, our world, our harvest field. God is still looking for men and women whom He can use. Not much has changed since Ezekiel penned those words in chapter twenty-two, verse thirty: *"And I sought for a man among them, that should make up the hedge, and stand in the gap before me for the land, that I should not destroy it."* Perhaps God will use the words you have read in this book to echo His plea found in Isaiah 6:8: *"I heard the voice of the Lord, saying, Whom shall I send, and who will go for us?"* Would you answer as Isaiah of old: *"Here am I; send me"*?

Becoming a laborer in God's harvest is just that— a labor! Revival is not easy and won't come to the faint-hearted or weak. I think of the words of Arnold Dallimore on the life of the great Evangelist George Whitefield:

> Although Whitefield himself spoke very little of the hardships he encountered, his "Journals" reveal the price he paid for the cause of Christ. His zeal and determination took him on an amazing course of evangelistic labor. After nine days of preaching in Philadelphia in the spring of 1740, he set out for New York. A seven-hour journey on horseback brought him to the home of Mr. Tennent at Neshaminy, where a congregation of 5,000 awaited him.

"When I got there (he writes) my body, through heat and labor was so weak and faint, that my knees smote one against another, my visage changed, and I was ready to drop down as soon as I had finished my prayer. But God was pleased to revive me. Great numbers were melted…." But despite his weakness, he traveled another eight miles that night and another sixteen the following morning. This brought him to the Dutch settlement of Shippack, where he reported:

Thursday, April 24… "It was seemingly a very wilderness part of the country but there were no less, I believe, than two thousand hearers… Traveling and preaching in the sun again, weakened me much and made me very sick; but by the Divine assistance, I took horse, rode twelve miles, and preached in the evening to about 3,000 people at a Dutchman's plantation…."

Friday, April 25. "Rose before day. Sang and prayed with my friends. Set out before sunrising, and reached Amwell, thirty-five miles from Shippack, where I was appointed to preach at six at night. Some thousands were gathered by noon awaiting my arrival. In my way thither, I was brought low by inward trials, and very great weakness of body, occasioned by the heat of the sun, want of sleep, and the length of the journey; but before I had preached six minutes, bodily and spiritual strength was given me, and the Lord set His seal to what He enabled me to deliver. After the sermon, a friend took me five miles to his house for rest."

But he was on his way again by eight o'clock the next morning and rode until four in the afternoon, in order to reach New Brunswick. He ministered there to 2,000 on Saturday evening and twice on Sunday to crowds of 7,000 and 8,000. On the Monday following, he reported that he "underwent great conflicts of soul last night and this morning," but he traveled and preached again the next day, and on Tuesday went on to New York.

In reference to these experiences, Dr. John Gillies wrote in *Memoirs of the Life of Reverend George Whitefield* published in 1772: "Sometimes he was almost dead with heat and fatigue. Thrice a day he was lifted upon his horse, unable to mount otherwise; then rode and preached, and came in and laid himself along two or three chairs."

John Foster in *Critical Essays* published in 1856, states: "Whitefield's career permitted him hardly a day of what could be called repose, till he found it in the grave at fifty-six.... We repeatedly find him, during a state of languor which sometimes sunk him quite down to illness, prosecuting such a course of exertions, as would have been enough to reduce most strong men to that condition; for example, preaching in his ardent and exhausting manner, to vast audiences, several times a day, a number of days successively, when his debility was such that he could not, without much help, mount his horse, to go to his appointed places. But his mind held such a predominance over his body, and the passion for preaching was so predominant in his mind, that as soon as he entered on preaching, he quickly became strong and animated."

Like many others in revival work, Whitefield was criticized, misunderstood, and falsely accused. His friends urged him to write about his life and ministry to set the record straight. He refused, however, and reminded his friends that God would keep track of the results. In fact, his tombstone at his own request, reads simply: "Here lies G.W. The record is on High."

May God raise up a generation of laborers who care more about revival than they do about the record!

Visit us online

strivingtogether.com

dailyintheword.org

wcbc.edu

lancasterbaptist.org

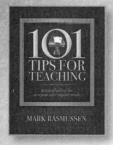
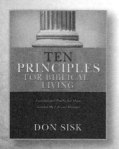
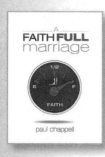